E. Lynn Linton

The true history of Joshua Davidson, Christian and communist

E. Lynn Linton

The true history of Joshua Davidson, Christian and communist

ISBN/EAN: 9783337733308

Printed in Europe, USA, Canada, Australia, Japan

Cover: Foto ©ninafisch / pixelio.de

More available books at **www.hansebooks.com**

THE TRUE HISTORY

OF

JOSHUA DAVIDSON

CHRISTIAN AND COMMUNIST

By E. LYNN LINTON

A NEW EDITION

London
CHATTO AND WINDUS, PICCADILLY

PREFACE TO THE SIXTH EDITION.

It would be affectation in me were I to pretend any longer to keep up the anonymity of the authorship of JOSHUA DAVIDSON. The secret has become known, as such secrets always do become known; and in one or two instances I myself was obliged to reveal it for the sake of truth and honesty. Now I come forward in my own person, prepared to take the full consequences of what I have written as Joshua's friend " John."

I would like to say a few words about the Communistic part of the book. Believing as I do, and as I think could be proved from the words of the Gospels as well as from the whole tenour of Christ's life, that pure Christianity, as taught by Him whom men

a

call God and Saviour, leads us inevitably to Communism, I carried my hero to the only modern scene where the central ideas were the rights of humanity against scientific arrangements, the raising of the low, the protection of the weak, the abasement of iniquity in high places, and the glorious liberty of this new Gospel preached to the poor.

(I may as well state here that, while acknowledging frankly its mistakes and misdeeds, I do not believe a tithe of the evil that was said of the Commune; just as I do not believe that the Jews ever roasted Christian babies for their Passover; or that the early Christians themselves celebrated the Last Supper by human sacrifices, or made of their Agapæ orgies of immorality.)

I did this because I wanted to bring the Christ of olden days into modern circumstances, and then to ask the respectable, the well-endowed, and the conservative Christians of to-day: How would they receive Him? How would they approve His doctrine? As I have said before, it is unreasonable to accept the words and deeds of Christ as of so arbitrary and final a character that they will not bear translation or analogy. What He was in the days of Herod He would be analogically in the reign of Victoria and under the rule of Napoleon. We have no right to deny this. Whatever there is of downtrodden, of degraded, of antagonistic to the existing order of things whereby the rich are made glad and the poor left miserable, the modern Christ would uphold and stand by. And perhaps not always with soft words. The curses hurled at Pharisee and Sadducee might, in those Parisian days, have expressed themselves in more tangible form; and a hierarchy clothed in purple and fine linen, a throne supported on bayonets, might not perhaps have seemed to Him so much deserving respect as a handful of poor enthusiasts, martyrs to their faith, opposing fire and sword to shot and shell.

I repeat again what I have said before, for it is a word that cannot be too often insisted on, that it is time for men to make their choice between absolute fidelity to the example of Him they say was God, absolute obedience to the word they believe to be the word of God, and a brave confession that this example is impossible to follow, and this word a proved misleading, therefore not divine. There is no middle course. It is Christianity and Communism, or the maintenance of the present condition of things as natural and fitting—that is,

the maintenance of the right of the strong
to hold, and the duty of the weak to submit.
In which case Christ came in vain for him
who believes; and was not God for him
who maintains as righteous the order of
society as we have it at this day. No man
who goes to the root of his faith, and cares
to look at it sincerely and without the haze
of an artificial atmosphere between him and
truth, can deny this position. If the alternative is terrible, the question is as momen-
tous; and anything would be better than
this fearful national hypocrisy, whereby we
confess a certain faith with our lips, and
absolutely refuse to translate it into practice.

I would also say, in answer to an accusation
more than once repeated, of having written
this book as a mere *jeu d'esprit*, that I
declare I have never written anything with
so much earnestness, such a passionate

desire to say out the truth as it seems to me; and that to enforce the supreme necessity of absolute sincerity between faith and practice, religion and social life, was the sole object I had in view.

E. Lynn Linton.

London, *June*, 1874.

PREFACE TO THE THIRD EDITION.

As JOSHUA DAVIDSON's biographer I have
been much perplexed by the various reviews
of my friend's life. Some have seen in it a
mere outflow of cant; others a parody of the
life of Christ; some have condemned it for
its bad political economy in holding that we
working men have wrongs, and that capital
has oppressed and does still heavily oppress
us; some for its sinful, others for its silly,
aim at that universal brotherhood and class
equalization which JOSHUA maintained to be
the logical political outcome of Christianity;
some have pronounced his life a failure
because of the weakness inherent in itself;
others, again, see in it a noble effort that
fell short of success by reason of the un-
christian state of Christendom. In fact, the

book has met with the same varied reception as did his work; and it is such as is given to all men who make bold to strip the veil from a convenient sham, and to force on the world the recognition of an unwelcome truth and the need of a disquieting decision.

No one wants to be troubled with logical Christianity. The idle ask only to be left in peace—things which did for their forefathers are good enough for them, and they hate the dust of cleaning-days; the rich do not wish their fat security to be endangered; the timid are afraid of new ways; the ingenious who have constructed a well-fitting puzzle by clever compromises despise the simplicity of first principles; sociologists deny the claims of individualism in favour of general laws; and all sectarians hold correct theological doctrine as more important than faithful imitative action. In the midst of these stand a few, earnest for absolute sincerity — and they have recognised the real meaning of JOSHUA's life ; and only they.

I go back on the question asked before, and not answered by one of the reviewers : Which is true, Science or Christ ? If Science, why then do we superstitiously hold to the letter of a faith whereof the spirit is dead ?—a faith, moreover, which preaches bad political economy and imperfect sociology all round :— If Christ, how can we delay another hour in translating His precepts and His practice, so passionately humanitarian as both were, into our own social and political action ? *The obstacles to practical Christianity come from professing Christians.* Let those who can, satisfactorily explain that phenomenon. For myself I am unable ; so was JOSHUA ; and one scarcely envies the subtle, shifty Œdipus who could.

Let us ask ourselves candidly what would be the manner of man, the course of action, and what the reception JESUS CHRIST would meet with, if He came among us now, in circumstances parallel to those of His own times. He would be a working man, and He would speak with a provincial accent; He would attack the capitalist, the political economist, the Sabbatarian, and the bench of bishops; He would live at the East End among the roughs and gaol-birds of Tiger Bay, who are our lepers, and He would denounce the luxury and respectability of the West End as He formerly denounced Dives and the Pharisees; He would teach the duty of indiscriminate charity, without inquiring too closely whether this man had sinned or his parents and the Board of Guardians, the Charity Organization Society, and the Mendicity people would, in turn, denounce Him; He would fraternize with the "enemies of society," as the discontented poor are called by those well endowed who fear to lose and refuse to share, with sinners, suspected persons, and all obscure and despised sects ; He would be unorthodox in faith, and a reformer in politics ; He would lecture in the Hall of Science ; and He would be, not crucified nor beheaded, but written down with the whole force of the press. It is not profane thus to realize the · life of Christ as a fact of the present day. He was a man, and He lived among men as one of themselves ; in a society as realistic and amidst class antagonisms as strong as our own. He was not a Voice from the Clouds, not a Burning Bush, not a mere Appearance : but a Reality, a Man ; and if His doctrine is divine, His acted life must be as divine. We have suffered our posthumous reverence to·

obscure by excess of worship the every-day aspect of His life ; and religious art has helped in this treacherous idealization. Still, we may fairly assume that the Man Christ Jesus was in outward seeming as other men ; that His divinity was to be discerned only by spiritual grace ; that He did not go about with a nimbus round His head, nor, as a new-born. infant, sit up straight and strong, and bless the kneeling kings. And we may as fairly assume that, were He to appear again under the same relative conditions as before, He would be no more recognised in Europe as the Messiah now than He was in Judea eighteen hundred years ago. The world has not changed in essential feeling since the days of Pontius Pilate and Barabbas. Still the leaders of popular thought, while despising the old, deny the new, and deliver it up to be scourged of ignorance, superstition,

and terrified Conservatism ; still the man of
expediency, who upholds current shams as
more convenient than truth and safer than
sincerity, is preferred to the man of lofty
theories, the enthusiast for noble ideas, him
we call Utopian, dreamer, or—Christ; still
the rich and the powerful hold their own
and gather more, while the poor and the
weak protest vainly against the inequality
of the division ; and still those who plead
the cause of the latter are the mark at which
the former shoot out their poisoned arrows.
If Christ has not died, neither has the Cross
been taken down ; and characters are crucified, if men are not.

Yet nothing of all this should daunt us.
It is our bounden duty to do what we can
for the Truth, and to fight against insincerity in all its forms.   We ought to
be brave enough in this day to dare ask

ourselves how much is practicable and how much impracticable in the creed we profess; and to renounce that which is even the most imperatively enjoined if we find that it is not wise or possible. If our religion leads us to political chimeras let us abjure it: if it teaches us truth let us obey it, no matter what social growths we tear up by the roots. There is no mean way for men. To slaves only should the symbols of a myth be sacred, and our very children are forbidden the weakness of knowing the right and doing the wrong. If such a man as JOSHUA DAVIDSON was a mistake, then acted Christianity is to blame. In which case, what becomes of the dogma? and how can we worship a life as divine the practical imitation of which is a moral blunder and an economic crime?

PREFACE.

So many false reports have got about concerning the life and opinions of JOSHUA DAVIDSON, the Cornish carpenter, that I feel it to be a duty I owe his memory to tell the truth as I know it; leaving the world to judge between what I, his nearest friend, knew of him, and what gossips and his enemies have falsely said. As I am neither a gentleman nor a scholar I have not pretended to any graces of style; and I have not tried to make an amusing story. My little book is more a record of what JOSHUA said and thought than of what happened to him through others: that is, there is next to no dramatic interest in it. Neither do I care to give my name. Those who know JOSHUA will know who I am well enough; and if I have said anything wrong they can come forward and challenge me. And for the rest it does not signify. I have written merely for truth's sake and love's; and with this I leave my dear friend's memory to the verdict of all honest hearts.

JOHN.

CHAPTER I.

JOSHUA DAVIDSON was the only son of a village carpenter, born in the small hamlet of Trevalga on the North Cornwall coast, in the year 1835. His parents were poor but worthy people, who kept themselves very much together and had but little to do with the neighbours. Folks blamed this for pride, and said they held themselves high because they were the decayed branches of an ancient family — some said dating from King Arthur's self. Of course this was only

B

an "Arthurian legend," if I may call it so,
that could not be verified; for naturally
down about Tintagel everything has to do
with King Arthur — even the choughs.
Joshua sometimes spoke of it, but not from
pride; there never was a man freer from
that failing than he; rather from the belief
he had in what a learned man would call
hereditary transmission, but as we say, just
"in the blood," and a kind of idea that
dawned on him, quite of late years, that
there would be a revival of national glories,
national names and leaders, under new
aspects but from the ancient sources. And
if so, might he not count for something,
direct descendant as he believed he was of
the hero whose Castle had been one of his
earliest playgrounds, and on whose Quoit he
had spent many an hour of way-side dream-

ing? It was a fancy; a harmless one; so
let it pass for just as much as it was
worth.

There was nothing very remarkable about
Joshua's childhood. He was always a quiet,
thoughtful boy, and from his earliest years
noticeably pious. His parents came of the
Friends' stock; not of a strict kind themselves, for they joined in the Church·services;
but the fact is just an indication of the kind
of influences which helped to mould him in
early youth. He had a habit of asking why,
and of reasoning out a principle, from quite a
little lad; which displeased people; so that
he did not get all the credit from the schoolmaster and the clergyman to which his dili-
gence and good conduct entitled him. They
thought him troublesome, and some said he
was self-conceited; which he never was; but

the more he was in earnest the more he offended them.

He was never well looked on by the Vicar since a famous scene that took place in the church one Sunday after afternoon catechism. He was then about fourteen years of age, and I have heard say he was a beautiful boy, with a face almost like a young woman's for purity and spirituality. He was so beautiful that some ladies and gentlemen staying at the Vicarage noticed him during church time, and said he looked like a boy-saint. But he knew nothing about himself. I question if he knew whether his hair was black like mine, or, as it was, a bright brown like ripe nuts in the sunshine. After catechism was over he stood out before the rest, just in his rough country clothes as he was, and said very respectfully to the

Vicar, Mr. Grand :* "If you please sir, I would like to ask you a few questions."

"Certainly, my lad, what have you to say?" said Mr. Grand rather shortly. He did not seem over well pleased at the boy's addressing him; but he could not well refuse to hear him because of the ladies and gentlemen with him, and especially Mr. Freeman, a very good old man who thought well of everybody, and let everybody do pretty much as they liked.

"If we say, sir, that Jesus Christ was God," said Joshua, "surely all that He said and did must be the real right? There cannot be a better way than His?"

---

* I do not mind giving this name of the clergyman, because it was not his own; only one that we lads gave him behind backs, as it were; else I do not intend to give the names of any living actors in this history. The scene I am now describing was told me by Joshua's mother, who wrote it down as soon as she got home.

"Surely not, my lad," Mr. Grand made answer; "what else have you been taught all your life? what else have you been saying in your catechism just now?"

"And His apostles and disciples, they showed the way too?" said Joshua.

"And they showed the way too, as you say; and if you come up to half they taught you'll do well, Joshua."

The Vicar laughed a little laugh as he said this; but it was a laugh, Joshua's mother said, that seemed to mean the same thing as a "scat"—our Cornish word for a blow—only the boy didn't seem to see it

"Yes; but, sir, it is not of myself I am thinking, it is of the world," said Joshua. "If we are Christians, why don't we live as Christians?"

"Ah indeed! why don't we!" said Mr.

Grand. "Because of the wickedness of the human heart; because of the world, the flesh, and the devil!"

"Then, sir, if you feel this, why don't you and all the clergy live like the apostles, and give what you have to the poor?" cried Joshua, clasping his hands and making a step forward, the tears in his eyes. "Why, when you read that verse, 'Whoso hath this world's good, and seeth his brother have need, and shutteth up his compassion from him, how dwelleth the love of God in him?' do you live in a fine house, and have grand dinners, and let Peggy Bray nearly starve in that old mud hut of hers, and widow Tregellis there, with her six children, and no fire or clothing for them? I can't make it out, sir! Christ was GOD; and we are Christians; yet we won't do as He ordered, though you tell us it is a sin that can never be forgiven if we dispute what the Bible says."

"And so it is," said Mr. Grand sternly. "Who has been putting these bad thoughts into your head?"

"No one, sir. I have been thinking for myself. Michael, out by Lion's Den, is called an infidel; he calls himself one; and you preached last Sunday that no infidel can be saved; but Michael helped Peggy and her base child when the Orphan Fund people took away her pension, because, as you yourself told her, she was a bad woman, and it was encouraging wickedness; and he worked early and late for widow Tregellis and her children, and shared with them all he had, going short for them many a time. And I can't help thinking, sir, that Christ, who forgave all manner of sinners, would have helped Peggy with her base child, and that Michael, being an infidel and such a good man, is something like that second son in the Parable who said he would not do his Lord's will when he was ordered, but who went all the same——"

"And that your Vicar is like the first?" interrupted Mr. Grand angrily.

"Well, yes, sir, if you please," said Joshua quite modestly but very fervently.

There was a great stir among the ladies and gentlemen when Joshua said this; and some laughed a little, under their breath because it was in church, and others lifted up their eyebrows, and said, "What an extraordinary boy!" and whispered together; but Mr. Grand was very angry, and said in a severe tone—

"These things are beyond the knowledge of an ignorant lad like you, Joshua; and I advise you, before you turn questioner and reformer, to learn a little humility and respect for your betters. I consider you have done a very impertinent thing to-day, and I shall mark you for it!"

"I did not mean to be impertinent, sir," said Joshua eagerly; "I want only to know the right of things from you, and to do as God has commanded, and Christ has shown us the way. And as you are our clergyman, and this is the House of God, I thought it the best plan to ask. I want only to know the truth; and I cannot make it out!"

"Hold your tongue, sir!" said Mr. Grand. "God has commanded you to obey your pastors and masters and all that are in

authority over you; so let us have no more
of this folly. Believe as you are taught,
and do as you are told, and don't set yourself up as an independent thinker in matters
you understand no more than the ass you
drive. Go back to your place, sir, and
another time think twice before you speak
to your superiors."

" I meant no harm. I meant only the
truth and to hear the things of God," repeated Joshua sadly, as he took his seat
among his companions; who tittered.

When they all went out of church Mr.
Grand was heard to say to Mr. Freeman :
" You will see, Freeman, that boy will go to
the bad; he will turn out a pestilent fellow,
a freethinker and a democrat. Oh, I know
the breed, with their cant about truth and the
right! He richly deserved a flogging to-day

if ever boy did; to dare to take me to task in my own church!"

But Mr. Freeman said gently; "I don't think he meant it for insolence. I think the lad was in earnest, though of course he should not have spoken as he did."

"Earnest or not, he must be taught better manners for the future," said Mr. Grand.

And so it was that Joshua was not well looked on by the clergyman, who was his enemy, as one may say, ever after.

All this made a great talk at the time, and there are many who remember the whole thing at this present day; as any one would find if they were to ask down at Trevalga; but all that Joshua was ever heard to say of it was: "I thought only of what was right in the sight of God; I never thought of man at all."

He did not however, repeat the experiment of asking inconvenient questions of his social superiors in public; but it was noticed that after this he became more and more thoughtful, and more and more under the influence of a higher principle than lads of his age are usually troubled with. And though always tender to his parents and respectful to the schoolmaster and minister, and the like of that, yet he was less guided by what might be called expediency in his conduct, and more than ever a stickler for the uncompromising truth, and the life as lived by Jesus Christ. He was not uncomfortable to live with, his mother said; quite the contrary; no one ever saw him out of temper, and no one ever knew him do a bad thing; but he somehow forced his parents to be always up to the mark, and even the neighbours were ashamed to talk loosely or say what they shouldn't before a lad whose whole thought, whose sole endeavour was, " how to realise Christ."

" Mother," he once said, as he and Mrs. Davidson stood by the cottage door together, " I mean when I grow up to live as our Lord and Saviour lived when He was on the earth. For though he is God in Heaven he was only man here ; and what He did we too can do with His help and the Holy Spirit's."

" He is our example, lad," said his mother reverently. " But I doubt lest you fall by over boldness."

" Then, if imitation is over bold, His life was a delusion, and He is not our example at all," said Joshua. " Which is a saying of the devil."

CHAPTER II.

JOSHUA did not leave home early. He wrought at his father's bench and was content to bide with his people. But his spirit was not dead if his life was uneventful. He gathered about him a few youths of his own age, and held with them prayer meetings and Bible readings, either at home in his father's house, or in the fields when the throng was too great for the cottage. It gave one a feeling as of old primitive times to be sitting there under the clear sky of a summer's evening, with the larks singing over head, and the swallows and sea birds flashing through the air, the voice of the waves as they beat up against Long Island subdued to a tender murmur that seemed to have a mystery somehow in it, and the young carpenter reading to us of Christ, and praying for the power to be like unto Him in life and heart; praying with an earnestness, a realization, a very passion of entreaty— nay, I have never heard or seen aught like it since, in church or chapel either!

And then he himself was so unlike other boys. He was so upright, so steadfast! No one ever knew Joshua tell the shadow of a lie, or go back from his word, or play at pretence. And he had such an odd way of coming right home to us. He seemed to have felt all that we felt, and to have thought all our thoughts. Young as he was, he was our leader even then. We all looked for great things from him. I should be laughed at if I said how high our expectations reached.

The youths that Joshua got together as his friends were as well-conditioned a set of lads as you would wish to see; sober, industrious, chaste. They were never in any trouble, and no one could say they had ever heard one of them give back a bad word, whatever the provocation, or say a loose one; but the clergy of their several parishes scouted them, and stood at no evil to say of them. For they were not church-goers; and that is always an offence to the clergy of country parishes, who treat even the best of the Dissenters as little better than rogues, taking it partly as a personal affront and partly as a moral sin if their parishioners find greater comfort for their poor souls elsewhere than under them. However, for the matter of that, the lads were of no denomination; and though they prayed much and often, it was neither at church nor chapel; it was at their own houses or in the fields.

Their aim was to be thorough and like Christ. They denounced the sin of luxury among professing Christians, and spared no one, lay or clerical: so did Christ, they said. They set their faces against the priestly class altogether, and maintained that Christ as High Priest needed no subordinate or go-between, and that the modern parson was only the ancient Pharisee, whom Christ was never weary of denouncing. They were anti-Sabbatarians too, as He had been, and held the doctrine of freedom in Christ throughout. They believed implicitly every word of the Gospels, which they stood by as

fuller of the Divine Life than the Epistles ,
and they thought that the Example left the
world was the one thing to follow and the
one pattern to imitate. Joshua's great hope
and desire, confessed among us, was to bring
back the world to the simplicity and broad
humanity of Christ's acted life; and as a
believer in the divinity of that life, he could
not understand how it had been let drop.
His one central point was the same now as
that which had formerly troubled him—and
Mr. Grand; namely, how, if Christ was God,
and His life given to us as our example, do
we not follow it literally, in simple exactness,
and as we find it set before us in the Gospels? And he believed that God would
strengthen his hands, not only to enable him
to realise this in his own person, but also to
evangelise society, and bring it over to the

Truth along with him.   He was waiting
for a Sign; and he believed it would be
given him.

He was but a young man at this time,
remember; enthusiastic, with little or no
scientific knowledge and with much of the
logic of fanaticism; unable to judge between
the possible and the impossible, and putting
the direct interposition of God above the
natural law.   Wherefore, he accepted the
text about faith removing mountains as
literally true, and possible to be done. Given
the faith, the mountain would move.   And
one evening he went down into the Rocky
Valley, earnest to try conclusions with God's
promise, and sure of proving it true. He had
fasted all day, and he had prayed all day;
not necessarily kneeling and repeating set
forms, but in the whole attitude of his mind;

and in the twilight when work was over he
went down with three of us, myself and two
others, all certain that the truth of the Word
would be made manifest, and that he could
remove rocks by FAITH.

He prayed to God to grant us this mani-
festation—to redeem His promise. He was
full of faith : not a shadow of doubt chilled
or slacked him. As he stood there in the
softening twilight, with his arms raised
above his head and his face turned up to
the sky, his countenance glowed as Moses'
of old. He seemed inspired, transported
beyond himself, beyond humanity. He
commanded the stone to move in God's
name, and because Christ had promised : and
we knelt beside him, not so much trembling
as exalted, feeling in the very presence of
the Divine, and that He would do unto us

according to His word. But the rock stood still; and a stonechat went and perched on it.

Another time he took up a viper in his hand, quoting the passage, "They shall take up serpents." But the beast stung him, and he was ill for days after. So, when he ate a handful of the berries of the black briony, and all but died of the poison. Yet he had handled the viper and eaten the berries in faith as simple and sincere as when he had commanded the stone in the Rocky Valley to move.

When the doctor was called in, and Joshua told him, boylike, what he had done and why and in what spirit, he shook his head gravely, and told his mother he was mad and had better be looked after.

"No, no, not mad, sir, because I believe

the Bible, and have determined to lead a life after Christ's word and example," said Joshua.

"Tut! rubbish!" said the doctor. "What you've got to do, my lad, is to plane your wood smooth and make your joists firm. All this religious folly of yours has no sense in it. I tell you it will upset your brain, and that you are mad now, and will be madder if you don't pull up in time."

"So Festus said to St. Paul, sir; but he was not mad, nor am I."

"But what do you want to do, jackass?" said the doctor with a good-humoured kind of impatience. "What's amiss with your poor foolish head that you can't take things easy?"

"I want to find out which is true, sir,"

answered Joshua: "the Bible which or-
dains certain ways of life; or the Christian
world which disobeys them. If Christ was
God, there is but one way for us all. He
could not have left us an imperfect example
to be mended here and there as we think
best for the convenience of society. He is
God or man; for, as things are, it is not
God and man—Christ and Christians; and
I want to know which is the truth."

"Take my advice," said the doctor
kindly; "put all these thoughts out of
your head as quickly as you can. Get
some work to do in a new part of the
country, fall in love with some nice girl,
and marry as soon as you can make a home
for her. Give over reading the Bible for a
time, and look up some pleasant stories and
books of travel, and the like; and leave off

eating poison-berries and handling vipers.
That's the only life for you, depend upon it;
and though I am no theologian, I venture
to say, that working honestly in that state
of life to which it has pleased God to call
you, going to church, keeping out of beer-
shops, and living like your respectable neighbours, is a far better kind of thing than
all this high-flown religion you are hanker-
ing after. Depend upon it, our best religion
is to do our duty, and to leave the care of
our souls to those whose business it is to
look after them."

" Thank you, sir ; you mean kindly,"
said Joshua. " But God has given me other
thoughts, and I must obey them if I would
not sin against the Holy Ghost."

And the doctor said afterwards to Mr.
Grand, that he was quite touched at the lad's

sweetness and wrong-headedness combined, and would have given much to have been able to send him there and then to a lunatic asylum, where he might have been taken care of for a time and put to rights.

The failure of these trials of faith perplexed us all, and profoundly afflicted Joshua. Not many men have gone through greater spiritual anguish, I should suppose, than he did at this time. It was like the sudden darkening of the sun to him, and the doubt of himself which it brought was nearer madness than his simple faith had been. He passed through a bad time; when his soul went down into the Valley of the Shadow, if ever man's did! But in time he came out into the light again. He knew his own sincerity, and his entire acceptance

of the Word of God and of the Divinity of
Christ; and he could not think that God
had met his prayer with a rebuff. God,
who knew the heart, would he felt sure
have accepted his endeavour, had that endeavour been within the scope of His plan
for humanity. It was the first struggle
between Faith and Law, Revelation and
Nature, through which every inquiring
mind has to pass; and it was a bitter
one.

He said nothing of these thoughts for
many weeks. He was not a youth who
jumped to conclusions, but rather one who
pondered well, and who let his thoughts
ripen; but at last he spoke one evening,
when we were gathered together as usual,
after work.

"Friends," he said, "it seems to me—

indeed. I think we must all see it now—
that His Word is not to be accepted literally, and not to be acted on in all its
details. The laws of Nature are supreme,
and even faith cannot change them. Can
it be," he then said solemnly, " that much
of that Word is a parable ?—that Christ
was truly as he says of Himself, the corner
stone, but not the whole building ?—and
that we have to carry on the work in His
spirit, but in our own way, and not merely
to try and repeat His acts ?"

I do not think we were prepared for such
a speech. We looked at one another un-
easily, even the dimmest of us seeing something of the conclusions to which such a
principle would lead us, and forecasting the
rudderless wandering of souls that would
ensue. But Joshua would say no more.

He bade us good-night soon after, and it
was long before we renewed the subject.
We all felt that he had broken dangerous
ground ; for had we not set out with the
determination to realise Christ in our lives,
founded on our conviction of the literal-
ness, the absolute uncompromising truth of
every word in the Gospels ?—a truth not to
be explained away, or paraphrased in any
manner of worldly wisdom or expediency ;
but to be accepted crude, naked, entire as
it is set down ? It was one thing or the
other—Christ or society, the Bible or the
world. It could not be both ; but once
admit the right of choice, of criticism, and
where was then our standard ? Yet again,
what could we make of that text about
faith, when we had proved it for ourselves
and found it wanting ? And if wrong in

ever so small a matter, was not our theory of absolute infallibility at an end? But if absolute infallibility was at an end, was not that making Christ a mere temporary teacher, local and for the day—not universal and for all time; and God a bit by bit worker? And if so, and even Gospel revelation is not final, where then exists the absolute necessity of acceptance? Yet, if we came to this conclusion—sorrowfullest of all!—we must relinquish all anchorage everywhere, and do our best to piece together a theory of life for ourselves, glad if any of the broken fragments of faith might still serve us.

But we were far off, as yet, from any such conclusions; and the Christ life, and the Gospel narrative, and the need laid on us all to follow in the Master's steps, and be-

lieve as He taught, and do as He did, were
still the cardinal points of Joshua's creed,
and the object of his endeavours : and, with
him, of ours.

CHAPTER III.

It was after this that we noticed a certain restlessness in Joshua. He seemed to feel the narrowness of his life down at such a dead place as Trevalga, where a man must work hard to keep body and soul together, and keep them very poorly when he has done his best; and where he cannot get forward save by his own thoughts. There is nothing for an energetic-minded young man to do there after his day's work is over. No lectures, no mechanics' institute, no library; only a few books to be borrowed here and there by chance. And Boscastle and Trevenna are no farther advanced; nor was even Camelford in those days. And then Camelford is full five miles away, across a wild whisht country that does not invite much night walking. To be sure there are the cliffs and the sea, the waterfall up at Knighton's Kieve, the rocks and the old ruins at Tintagel—King Arthur's Castle—which fill the imagination. But imagination does very well for extreme youth, as looking back does for old age: a man coming to his prime wants action.

An opening however came in time, and Joshua had an offer to go up to London to follow his trade at a large house in the City; which he accepted; and got me a job as well, that I might be alongside of him. For we were like brothers; he, the elder, the better, the leader; and I, the younger, the led. And neither was afraid of work; or, let me add, afraid for our work. We were skilled in our trade so far as we could be without first-rate teaching, having made it a point of duty and honour both, that we should never give folks occasion to talk of us as babbling saunterers, who took to the Bible because they could not manage the plane and the saw.

A few days before he went, Joshua happened to be coming out of his father's workshop just as Mr. Grand was passing, driving the neat pair-horse phaeton he had lately bought.

"Well, Joshua, and how are you doing?" said the parson, pulling up.

I dare say he was a good man when he was at home, but Mr. Grand was not fit to be a parish priest—at all events, not of such a place as Trevalga. He might have made a fine general officer, or a dignitary in a cathedral where he had nothing to do with the poor; but among a lot of half-starving, uneducated creatures, such as you find in a by-kind of coast hamlet in Cornwall, he was worse than useless. He had no love for the poor, and no pity : he always called them "the common people," and spoke of them disdainfully, as if they were different creatures from gentry. I question if he allowed us the same kind of souls ; and I do know that he denied equality of condition after death, and quoted the text of "many mansions" in proof of his theory of exclusion. He was a man of good family himself, and his wife was the daughter of a bishop ; he was rich too, and looked to be made dean or bishop himself by time. So you see, Trevalga was only a stopping-place with him, where he just put off the time the best way he could till he saw his way to better things; and he didn't care a rush for any one in the place.

However, he drew up at seeing Joshua, and asked him how he was; and then said: "And why have you not been to church lately, my man?" as if Joshua had been in the habit of going, and had failed only of late. This was Mr. Grand's way. He never knew anything about his people. That gave them to think, you see, that he held himself too high to notice what such poor wretches might be about. God forgive me if I misjudge him!

"Well, sir," said Joshua, "I don't go to church, you know."

"No? have you joined the chapel then? Is that your latest fad, Joshua?"

"No, sir; neither church nor chapel," answered Joshua.

"What! a new light on your own account, hey?" and he laughed as if he mocked him.

"No, sir, only a seeker."

"The old paths not good enough for you?—the light that has lightened the Gentiles these eighteen hundred years and more not pure enough for an unwashed Cornish lad, planing wood at a carpenter's bench, and not able to speak two consecutive words of good English?"

"I must answer for my conscience to God, sir," said Joshua.

"And your clergyman, appointed by God and the State to be your guide, what of him? Has he no authority in his own parish?" cried Mr. Grand warmly. "Does it never strike you, my fine fellow, that in thinking for yourself, as you call it, you are flying in the face both of Divine ordinances and the laws of man, and that you are entering on the sin of schism on the one hand, and of rebellion on the other ? "

" Look here, sir," said Joshua with earnestness, but quite respectfully ; " if I speak plainly, I mean it for no offence; but my heart burns within me and I must speak out. I deny your appointment as a God-given leader of souls. The Church is but the old priesthood as it existed in the days of our Lord, and is, as much as that was, the blind leading the blind. There are good and kind gentlemen among you, but not Christians according to Christ. I see no sacrifice of the world, no brotherhood with the poor——"

" The poor ! " interrupted Mr. Grand disdainfully; " what would you have, you young fool ? The poor have the laws of their country to protect them, and the Gospel preached to them for their salvation."

" Yes, and in preaching that—that is, in giving two full services on Sundays, and reading the marriage-service and the burial-service and the like of that when you are wanted—you discharge your conscience of all other obligations towards them, and think you have done enough. You never seem to remember that when Christ preached the Gospel to the poor it was to make them equal with the rich. Why, sir, the poor of our day are the lepers of Christ's ; and who among you, Christian priests, consorts with them ? Who ranks the man above his station, or the soul above the man ? "

"Now, we have come to it!" cried Mr. Grand. "I thought I should touch the secret spring at last! And you would like us to associate with you as equals?—Is that it, Joshua? Gentlemen and common men hob-and-nob together, and no distinctions made? You to ride in our carriages, and perhaps marry our daughters?"

He had his little girl of six or so in the phaeton with him; a pretty little maid that used to go about dressed in blue velvet and a white feather in her hat.

"That's just it, sir. You are gentlemen, as you say, but not the followers of Christ. If you were, you would have no carriages to ride in, and your daughters would be what Martha and Mary and Lydia and Dorcas were, women of no station, bent only on serving God and the saints, and their title to ladyhood founded on their degrees of goodness."

"Going in for socialism, Joshua?" said Mr. Grand, continuing his bantering tone. "A little radicalism, a little methodism, and a great deal of self-assurance—that seems to me to be about where you are!"

"Going in for no isms at all, sir," said Joshua. "Only for the truth as it is in Christ!"

"Shall I tell you what would be the very thing for you?" said Mr. Grand quite quietly.

"Yes, sir; what?" asked Joshua eagerly.

"This whip across your shoulders!—and, by George, if I were not a clergyman I would lay it there, with a will!" cried the parson, half rising from his seat.

No one had ever seen Joshua angry since

he had grown up. His temper was pro-
verbially sweet, and his self-control was a
marvel. But this time he lost both. It was
not so much as a man, because of the insult
to himself; he would have borne that meekly
enough ; but it was the feeling that the
Sacred Thing had been mocked in him which
drove him into sudden anger: an anger so
violent and so sudden as to take the
clergyman fairly aback.

"God shall smite thee, thou whited wall!"
he cried with vehemence. "Is this your
boasted leadership of souls?—this your learned
solving of difficulties?—this your fatherly
guidance of your flock? 'Feed my lambs'
—with what? with stones for bread—with
insult for sincerity—with the gentleman's
disdain for the poor thought of the artisan
—with class insolence for spiritual diffi-

culties! Of a surety, Christ has to come again to repeat the work which you priests and churches have destroyed and made of no effect, and to strip you of your ill-used power. You are the gentleman, sir, and I am only a poor carpenter's son; but I stand against you now—man against man—soul against soul—and I spurn you with a deeper and more solemn scorn than you have spurned me!" He lifted his hand as he said this, with a strange and passionate gesture, then turned himself about and went in; and Mr. Grand drove off more his ill-wisher than before; as perhaps was only natural. And yet he richly deserved all he had got.

This was one of the stories that got bruited abroad to Joshua's discredit. Some said he had struck the parson—some that he

had been monstrously and unjustifiably impertinent; and the tale got bandied about as
a kind of dramatic scarecrow—a kind of
logical warning to young men given to think
for themselves, as to what would become of
them if they shook themselves free of authority. "You'll be as bad as Joshua to Parson
Grand," was a phrase I myself heard more
than once. But here is the story just as it
happened; and I put it to my readers—was
Joshua so very much to blame, all things
considered—motives, feelings, spiritual disappointment, and that inner dignity of Man
which overpowers all social differences when
the fit moment comes? I can only say that
never, to the last, could he be got to see that
he had done wrong, and never, to the last,
could I say it or see it either.

"No," he used to say, "some kinds of

anger are righteous; and this was of them."

But Mr. Grand made old Davidson, Joshua's father, suffer for his son; for he took away his own custom from him, and did him what harm in the neighbourhood a gentleman's ill-word can do a working man. It was a bad thing for the old man. The Trevalga schools were being built, and St. Juliot's church was under repair, and Davidson, as the best workman thereabouts, would have been sure to have been head man at both jobs. But Mr. Grand, he put his spoke in that wheel; and one day when I took courage to speak and plead, all I got was a recommendation to mind my own business, and not interfere where I was not wanted. And then as if in consideration—a kind of condescending consideration—for my being a "canter," Mr. Grand wound up with saying that I must see he was justified according to the law of God.

When I challenged him hotly, I daresay intemperately, I daresay even impertinently, for his proof—for you see I was but a poor uneducated artisan, and he was a gentleman and a scholar—he laughed, and said he did not argue with carpenters' lads; and when I answered back, he ordered me out of the house, saying I was as pestilent a fellow as my friend;—I replying angrily that I did not think the pestilence rested with Joshua. Which ended the interview; not without loss of temper and dignity on both sides, and no good done to anyone.

The night before we left for London Joshua had a kind of vision or waking dream, which he told me as we were on our way to Launceston, walking up the hill from Boscastle, while the omnibus toiled after us. He was on the cliff by Long Island, when suddenly he seemed to be caught away to a wide plain, where many men were gathered. In the centre of the plain was a hill, like Brown Willy out there by Camelford, and on this hill sat two kingly figures who ruled over the swarming multitudes below. They sat together hand in hand, and he saw that they were in some mysterious manner inseparable. The one was dressed as a high priest, and was Ecclesiastical Christianity; the other as a king, and was Society; and both were stern, forbidding, and oppressive. The only persons to whom they showed favour were the well-dressed and the subservient—rich people dressed in gold and jewels, and

the poor and undistinguished who were
submissive and conforming ; who accepted all that the high priest taught
without questioning the truth of any part,
and who obeyed what the king ordained
without even so much as a wish to resist.
These were called Believing Christians and
Respectable Members of Society ; and, in
consideration of their obedience, both the
high priest and the king smiled on them, and
spoke them fair. Yet they were scarcely
friendly to their adherents. The one surrounded them with the most monstrous
shapes of demons cast by magic lanterns
and in every way unreal, of which they were in
continual fear—GOD, whom yet they labelled
"Our Father," and the "God of Love,"
the most terrible looking demon of all ; and
the more they were afraid, and the more

cruel they believed Our Father to be, the more Ecclesiastical Christianity was content. The other bound them round and round with chains and swathing bands, till they were scarcely able to move or breathe. And when they submitted to the stifling torture with a good grace—some of them even drawing the links tighter, and buckling up the thongs more home of their own accord, and all declaring the pattern of each particular bandage to have been sent down direct from heaven, and in no wise invented as an experiment by Society—then the king smiled on them kindly, and praised them with many flattering words; and the poor atrophied wretches were quite content with the barren honour of their reward.

At the feet of these two rulers lay three figures cruelly bound and tortured. They

E

were Truth, bearing in her arms her young child Science, Freedom, and Humanity. All three were stretched on racks made in the form of a cross, which gave in the eyes of the multitude a kind of symbolic sanction to their torture. The two rulers were for ever trying to gag them, so that they should not speak ; but they could not quite succeed ; and every now and then they uttered words, loud and clear as the sound of a silver trumpet, that stirred the multitude below, and set men running hither and thither, some shaking themselves free of the bonds in which both Christianity and Society had bound them. And when they spoke, the high priest and the king and their worshippers, all the well-dressed little kings and poorer conformists, buffeted them ; and would have killed them if they could.

Ill-treated as they were however, each tortured being had a small knot of adherents. Round Truth, bearing her young child, Science, gathered men of imposing aspect—men of authority, of large brains, of temperate nature, of clear and candid thought. There were some among them of such unquestionable grandeur, that even the mob of Believing Christians and Respectable Members of Society paid them a certain cold, deprecatory reverence as they passed; while Ecclesiastical Christianity tried to reconcile their statements with his own creed, hiding his magic lantern painted with demons and that all-devouring hell with which he terrified the multitudes, when he spoke to them; saying, "See, there is no such great difference between us after all! I do not contradict you. Say what you will about the sun, and the age of the earth, the relations of the universe, and the gradual evolution of man, nothing that you advance disturbs me. I only supplement you, and add the divine grace of spiritual truth, which is beyond your analysis. You are right and I am right; let us be friends and brothers."

Society was less concerned about these philosophers. They were for the most part swathed in *his* bands tight enough; some for pre-occupation with other matters, some for expediency, some for dread of the unknown, and some for conviction; and, for the rest, he let his twin-brother, the high priest, fight his battles as he best could.

Round the prostrate form of Freedom, scarred, gashed, bleeding, fettered, stood only a few. Even the men of science were afraid of this huge giant, this son of the old gods, whose might no one had been able to calculate should he once arise in his strength. All, save his own few lovers, chiefly of the poorest class, looked on him with dread, and prophesied evil days for the world should he ever get free of his bonds and the symbolic constraint of the cross. But his small band of lovers, themselves either martyrs or victims, worked incessantly at his deliverance; every now and then getting one link loosened here and another there, knowing that in time he would with their help shake himself free of all his chains, and stand up before the world, the great-hearted leader, the glad possession of every man and woman that breathes.

The third figure was the most deeply oppressed. The face was hidden, but it was

a lovely form, vilely clad in disfiguring garments, and bespattered with dirt that had
been flung at it by the high priest and
Society in concert. On its nailed hands
hung the weeping and the miserable; and
no one was rejected or bidden back. The
most miserable sinner that crawled—the
thief, the murderer, the harlot—it gathered
them all around it: its own bound hands
doing their checked best to free them from
their stains. Pleasure and pain and sin and
virtue all rested equally on its large breast,
and to all it gave full sympathy and understanding. It condemned no one; only it
refused obedience to the high priest and the
king. As the dreamer looked, it slowly
turned its face to the sky: and Joshua recognised in the soiled and vilified face of
Humanity—the face of Christ.

Suddenly standing side by side with the magnificently attired pontiff, this Ecclesiastical Christianity, oppressor of Truth, slanderer of Humanity, tyrant of Freedom, ruler of the churches, and through them of the consciences of men ; side by side too, with his twin-brother Society, his fellow-tyrant and oppressor, was a man coarsely clad in rude garments, a man of uncultured speech, of unconventional manners, but of a noble aspect, whose face was the face of an enthusiast who believed in himself, and in whose self-reliance were his sole credentials. His companions were the same as those who had gathered round the crucified form of Humanity. All the poor and the miserable, the leprous, the sinners, the outcast, and those "sinless Cains" of history, those men who had lived to do good

to their generation, and who had been stoned
and crucified and blasphemed and cursed as
their reward—they were all clustered closely
round him. He had nothing to do with
that regal Society, that mitred Christianity.
He loudly proclaimed his antagonism to
both, and drew to him only such as they
spurned and rejected.

He pointed to the high priest : " Look,"
he said to Joshua, " what they have made of
me ; of an unskilled artisan, no schoolman even
of his day, and a vagrant preacher living by
charity, they have made a king ; of a man, a
god ; of a preacher of universal tolerance,
the head of a persecuting religion ; of a life,
a dogma ; of an example, a church. Here
am I, Jesus the Nazarene, the son of Joseph
and Mary, as I lived on earth ; poor, unlearned, a plebeian, and a socialist, at war

with the gentlemen and ladies of my society, the enemy of forms, of creeds, of the priestly class of respectabilities ; and there you see my modern travesty, this jewelled, ornate, exclusive Ecclesiastical Christianity, who is the ancient Pharisee revived. To you, and to such as you, is given the task of bringing men back to the creed that I preached. And if in securing the essence of the creed you forget the Founder, and call my doctrine by another name than mine, so be it. The world wants the thing, not the label ; and Christ-likeness, not Ecclesiastical Christianity, is the best Saviour of men."

As he said this the whole vision seemed to fade away, and the voice of Peggy Bray, whining and drunk, with Mr. Grand's deep tones of angry disgust, broke the quiet evening stillness, and brought Joshua back to the realities of life.

"Something seemed to bid me," he said, when he told me the story: "I ran off over the down as fast as I could, and caught Peggy on the Tintagel Road. She was drunk, dirty, and crying. I took her by the hand. 'Peggy, woman,' I said, 'dry your eyes, and come along with me.' I spoke so sudden, I startled her, and so a little sobered her. Then I took her by the arm and led her to mother's cottage. 'Here, mother,' I said; 'here is a bit of Christ-work for you to do. Take this poor creature, in her dirt and vileness as she is, and cleanse her. You believe and know that God's love did that for the world: we are less pure than Christ, but we hold ourselves too fine to follow His example in that! Love her, mother; she is your sister—and maybe your love can heal her.' Poor mother! she didn't like the task. She cried over it, and said that I put a burden on her she could not bear; but I held to my point," said Joshua, with a glowing face; "and she yielded. Peggy stayed in our house for over a month, and mother was ill-called for her work. Not that she much cared, I fancy. I don't know, however, whether she did or not; she never said much. And though Peggy broke out again and went to the bad as before, yet a month's experience of loving-kindness and cleanly living was something. At all events, it was practical Christianity; and if it did Peggy herself little or no good permanently, it was the right thing to do, and mother was so far benefited."

CHAPTER IV.

In London a new view of life opened to
Joshua altogether. The first thing that
struck him in our workshop was the avowed
infidelity of the workmen, with the indifference so many of them showed for any
spiritual life at all. Having apparently made
up their minds that Christianity, as taught by
the churches and practised in high places, is
a humbug throughout, they seemed to have
stopped there, not caring to go farther, nor
to find a truer and better religion for themselves. Distrust had penetrated to their in-

most souls, and God was abandoned because man had betrayed them. Some of the better class among them had become Unitarians; which gave them the most religion with the least dogma of all the sects that go by the name of Christian; and some had transferred their whole passion and life of thought and intellectual energy to science, finding that consolation in nature which they could not get from revelation. But very few were what is called religious men : that is, men believing in the Bible, going to church on Sundays, and reverencing the clergy as men placed over them by a higher power to guide their souls as they would.

The immense gulf existing between the church and the workmen also surprised the Cornish lad. At home, though the cottagers and the clergy stood as wide as the poles apart, socially and intellectually, yet there was some kind of mutual knowledge and intercourse; which, if it meant little for human wants and less for spiritual needs, still was intercourse and knowledge. In London there was none; or so little in proportion to the work to be done, it seemed almost as good as none. The parish priest, save in some chiefly ritualistic exceptions, scarcely exists, and his place is supplied by all sorts of lieutenants, both authorised and irregular; by Bible women, the City missionaries, Baptists, Roman Catholics, and the thousand and one odd, obscure sectaries of whom no one in good society ever heard the names — anything rather than the fashionable preacher who has invested all his store of godliness in his sermons, or the beneficed clergyman who thinks his East-end income dearly bought at the price of his East-end residence.

As he grew however, to understand the inner relations of life in the metropolis, he ceased to wonder at the wide-spread indifferentism of the working men; and he came further to understand how religion, like other things, had followed that class antagonism felt by the artisan, to which the exclusiveness of caste cherished by the rich had given birth. Christianity represents to the poor, not Christ tender to the sinful, visiting the leprous, the brother of publicans, at whose feet sat the harlots and were comforted, but the bishop in his palace and the parson in his grand house, the gentleman taking sides with God against the poor and oppressed, as an elder brother in the courts of heaven kicking the younger out of doors. It is in fact, he used to say, antagonism not love; Cain not Christ.

His religious experiences followed the natural course of such a mind as his, at once so earnest and so logical. Attracted by the self-sacrificing lives of so many of the Ritualist party, he threw himself with ardour into the congregation of a noted City priest whose name I do not feel justified in giving, as I have not asked his consent. If, however, he should read these pages he will remember Joshua Davidson well enough. The Superior, as he was called, took to him greatly, and Joshua felt all the charm of close intercourse with a cultivated mind. It was the first time this great good had been granted him, and it was like a new life to him. At one time I thought he would have abandoned the independent line he had chosen and would have gone over to the High Church party; but I do not think now that he was ever very near. For, fascinated as he was with the earnestness and culture of the Superior and his colleagues, they failed to hold him mainly because of the largeness of their assertions, the smallness of their proofs, and the feeling he had that more lay behind their position than they acknowledged, and that they used their adherents as tools. Added to which, their devotion to the Church rather than to Christianity at large, the absorption of the human example of Christ in His mystical character, the deification of the man as He lived, as if He had walked about like a God with a halo round His head, and was not a real man of the people of his time— of lowly birth, of confessed scientific ignorance, in antagonism to all the wealth and

r

culture, and class-refinement and political economy of His day, fighting the cause of the poor against the rich, of the outcast against the aristocrats, just as any earnest democrat, any single-hearted communist, might be doing at the present day—all this repelled him from close union ; and all this made him feel that, great and good as the men themselves are, in the High Church movement was not his Shekinah. Then again, their elaborate system of symbolism seemed to him puerile ; a playing with spiritual toys that had less reality than ingenuity ; and their central creed of sacrifice rather than commemoration in the Eucharist, backed by their assumption of a priesthood possessing unproved and mysterious powers, failed to convince him.

"You have captivated my heart," he one

day said to the Superior—"you charm my tastes—you delight my imagination; but you have not mastered my reason. Fairly reasoned out I do not think your position is tenable. You are Roman Catholics under another name; irregulars claiming to be received on the footing of the acknowledged Body Guard; you are infallible yet eclectic, and I cannot concede infallibility to eclecticism."

"But have you no reverence for the virtues of obedience and humility?" asked the Superior. "Cannot you quell that questioning spirit of yours for the sake of the Church's honour, and to maintain a close front? Who can hope to do anything as an isolated unit against a host? Is not the whole secret of strength in organisation?"

"But I cannot become part of a system

for expediency!" said Joshua mournfully. "Some men may, but it is not given to me to be able to stifle my own individual conscience for any considerations of party strength. I have got it to do—to find out if practical Christianity is possible in the world, and to learn why, being Christians, we are not of Christ. I know I should get something of the kind in such institutions as St. Vincent de Paul and the like, but I should have there so much in excess of the simple faith I love, that I cannot join them. I must go on my way alone."

"And you will fail," said the Superior. "No one man can succeed in such a search as yours. Guided by wise counsels and supported by authority you might come to satisfactory conclusions; but adrift on the wide sea of dissent, and private opinion, and individual interpretation, you are **lost**. To the Church came the promise and the Spirit; believe me the Church is your only ark."

"If any, then the Roman Catholic at once, frankly and without reserve," said Joshua. "If the keys of life and death are held by a governing body, they are surely held within the Vatican; and if I must enter into the virtue of unquestioning obedience, I would rather accept it in its totality. Your ritualism seems to me like Canute and the waves. 'Thus far and no farther,' you say to private inquiry; and 'only so much and so much will we take of tradition and the vitality of past ages.' Where is your standing-point? where your logical foothold? By what authority do you reject and accept at will? and by what measure do you set the length of the tether of reason ? "

" If you are for the whole history of the Church you must read more closely than you have done," said the Superior a little evasively.

" Forgive me, sir," continued Joshua earnestly ; " I know you will, whatever I say ; for I am speaking now heart-open, man to man, and there is no question of discourtesy or of courtesy ; but with all my personal love and admiration for the professors of your creed, the creed itself is tainted with an insincerity I cannot digest. And your position, standing as you do in the front, between yearning souls demanding the support of authority, the moral protection of infallibility, and the only Western Church that can give it logically, is, to my

way of thinking, both dangerous to your-
selves and cruel to the people. Why do
you not go over to Rome at once, sir, since
your commission is self-appointed and irregular?"

The Superior smiled gently. "I never
argue," he said; "for I never found any
good to come of it. These questions are
matters for spiritual reception, not dialec-
tical discussion. Use the appointed means
and the grace of our Lord will find
you."

"I have used them; I do use them; and
yet I cannot get conviction," Joshua made
answer, as sorrowfully as frankly.

"Persevere!" said the Superior solemnly;
"the promises of God never failed yet."

Joshua did not speak. He remembered
his trial of the material promises and how

they failed; but he did not go into that
with the Superior.   He had learnt to look
back on the phase through which he had
passed then as a boyish craze, sincere if you
will, but a craze all the same.   Yet it had
struck into him, and, perhaps unknown to
himself how much, had helped greatly to
modify his views.   It had broken down his
belief in the literal exactness of the Scrip-
tures, and the science-lectures he attended
went the same way; and when one's child-
like confidence has received its first shock,
it is long before anything like an analogous
faith is reconstructed out of more mature
knowledge.

At this time Joshua's mind was like an
unpiloted vessel.   He was beset with
doubts, in which the only thing that kept
its shape or place was the character of

Christ. For the rest, everything had failed him.

"What," he said to me at this time, "if the spiritual life is as little real as that act of faith in which we all failed?— if what we call conviction is only a state of the mind—a subjective condition owning no absolute without—a state as good and righteous for the Buddhist, for the Mohammedan, for the Hindoo, as for the various Christian denominations? We are all convinced. Every creed has had its martyrs and enthusiasts and its well-trained, well-balanced professors, all as firmly convinced of its truth and of its being the one truth only, as the Superior is convinced of the absolute rightness of Anglicanism, as the Pope believes in the infallibility of his Church, and the whole Christian world in the impregnability of the Bible and its literal exactness. I cannot focus God as these men are able to do; and yet I feel it better to be rooted than wandering, as I am wandering now, unfixed and unnourished. If you are rooted you can grow; but floating, hovering, what is the soul but as one of those winged seeds carried about by the wind and fastened nowhere?"

"And yet," I answered, "it is better to be unfastened from a fallacy than to be rooted on it. There must be the moment of suspension when you are in progress. To mount a ladder you must leave the rung on which you stand, and before you have your foot on the other it is nowhere—only in space. The time of doubt is a time of pain, but it must be passed through if we would believe the better thing. To have lost the old land-marks—left them behind us—is not necessarily to have lost the right way, Joshua!"

"Ah! but to have been so near to God as I once felt myself—to have lived in the light —and now to be so far off—to be in darkness and alone!" he sighed.

"The darkest hour is that before dawn," was my reply. "Even at this moment God may be preparing you for conviction."

I do not think that what is called the Evangelical school ever warmed Joshua as the Ritualists had done. If the assumptions of the Church, clad in her venerable authority, seemed to him excessive, the assumptions of sectarianism, where each man is an independent pope and quite as bigoted as the real one, were more so. And he could not come to believe that faith, which is a thing we cannot give ourselves, which will not come for the seeking, and which, when we have it, is as likely to lead us wrong as right—unless all beliefs are true alike; which sectarianism does not admit—is the one sole means of salvation, without which we are lost. It seemed to him a theory entangled in contradictions. Faith is the gift of God; no one can believe at will, but only as God gives him grace to do so; but if you do not believe you are damned, and God punishes you for not having what He will not bestow. Again, you have to distinguish between your various kinds of faith, and you must discern accurately which kind is sent by God and which by the devil. No outward test can tell you: for the Calvinist holds the Romanist in deadly error; the Romanist damns the heretic with no hope of mercy; the Anglican talks about the deadly sin of dissent; and not one of them all regards the Unitarian, the Jew, or the Pagan, as in any sort of possibility a child of God, or as aught but a confirmed, if unconscious, son of the devil. What known test then can be applied to all these conflicting schools? To Joshua's mind, none; and the more he sought for the unerring truth—truth centralised, unified, focussed—the less, it seemed to him, he found it, and the more dignity and grandeur and charity he felt resided in the wide creed of Universalism.

During this time he did not neglect what I suppose may be called secular life. He attended all such science-classes as he had time for; and being naturally quick in study, he picked up a vast deal of knowledge in a

very short time; he interested himself in
politics, in current social questions, specially
those relating to labour and capital, and in
the condition of the poor. This, above all,
was his main subject; and perhaps more
than any thing else, the fact that all the
sects and denominations he had searched
into accepted the class divisions of the present time as final, and thought that it was
enough to preach the Gospel to the poor—
that is, to preach to them submission and
patience, and belief that Christ was God,
and then leave them to their physical
wretchedness and social degradation as to
things that must be, and with which they
must make themselves content—had turned
him from communion with them, one and
all. It was such a comfortable way of getting rid of a difficulty, he used to say. It

was offering a potential heaven as a bribe to induce the starving and the down-trodden to be patient with their sufferings, and submissive to the unjust tyranny of circumstances. It was shirking the question of Christian equality altogether, and nullifying the whole teaching and tendency of Christ's life.

So his time passed, and his thoughts went more and more into the rationalistic channel; till at last one evening, when I and other of his friends were sitting with him, he made his declaration.

"Friends," he said, "I have at last cleared my mind and come to a Belief. I have proved to myself the sole meaning of Christ: it is Humanity. I relinquish the miracles, the doctrine of the Atonement, the doctrine of the Divinity of Jesus, and the

unelastic finality of His knowledge. He
was the product of His time; and if He
went beyond it in some things, He was
only abreast of it in others. His views of
human life were oriental; His images are
drawn from the autocratic despotism of the
great and the slavish submission of the
humble, and there is never a word of repro-
bation of these conditions, as conditions, only
of the individuals according to their desert.
He did His best to remedy that injustice, so
far as there might be solace in thought, by
proclaiming the spiritual equality of all men,
and the greater value of worth than status;
but He left the social question where he found
it—paying tribute even to Cæsar without re-
luctance—His mind not being ripe to accept
the idea of a radical revolution, and His hands
not strong enough to accomplish it, if even

He had imagined it. But neither He nor His disciples imagined more than the communism of their own sect; they did not touch the throne of Cæsar, or the power of the hereditary irresponsible Lord. Their communism never aimed at the equalization of classes throughout all society. Hence, I cannot accept the beginning of Christian politics as final, but hold that we have to carry on the work under different forms. The modern Christ would be a politician. His aim would be to raise the whole platform of society, he would not try to make the poor contented with a lot in which they cannot be much better than savages or brutes. He would work at the destruction of caste, which is the vice at the root of all our creeds and institutions. He would not content himself with denouncing sin as merely spiritual evil: he would go into its economic causes, and destroy the flower by cutting at the roots—poverty and ignorance. He would accept the truths of science, and he would teach that a man saves his own soul best by helping his neighbour. That, indeed, He did teach ; and that is the one solid foothold I have. Friends, Christianity according to Christ is the creed of human progress, not that of resignation to the avoidable miseries of class ; it is the confession that society is elastic, and that no social arrangements are final ; that morals themselves are only experimental, and that no laws are divine—that is, absolute and unchangeable by circumstance. It is the doctrine of evolution, of growth ; and just as Christ was the starting-point of a new era of theological thought, so is the present the starting-point of a new era of social fact.

Let us then strip our Christianity of all the mythology, the fetichism that has grown about it. Let us abandon the idolatry with which we have obscured the meaning of the Life; let us go back to the MAN, and carry on His work in its essential spirit in the direction suited to our times and social conditions. Those of you who still cling to the mystical aspect of the creed, and who prefer to worship the God rather than imitate the Man, must here part company with me. You know that, as a youth, I went deep into the life of prayer and faith; as a man, I have come out into the upper air of action; into the understanding that Christianity is not a creed as dogmatised by churches, but an organization having politics for its means and the equalization of classes as its end. It is Communism. Friends! the doc-

trine I have chosen for myself is Christian
Communism—and my aim will be, the Life
after Christ in the service of humanity,
without distinction of persons or morals.
The Man Jesus is my master, and by His
example I will walk."

CHAPTER V.

THESE then were the stages through which Joshua's mind had passed; first, literal acceptance of the Word, which as he went on he found to be against the laws of nature, and which therefore he relegated to the ignorance and exaggeration of the time in which it was written; next, the authority of the Church with its increment of symbolism and tradition, by which the Humanity of Jesus is resolved into a mystical Appearance of Divinity, and his Life made no longer an example for men to follow but a dogma to be worshipped under emblems ; and now the frank acceptance of that Humanity alone, of the Man as a teacher, and of the Life as an example to be faithfully followed ; more especially in its tenderness to sinners and its brotherhood with the poor and outcast. It was an abandonment of the dead mystical for the living real ; but I doubt if any single sect among all the hundreds into which the Christianity of Jesus is shredded, would have recognised him as a brother Christian, or have believed that Christ would do aught else to him in the Last Day but deny him as a " thief and a robber."

And now Joshua began to carry out his programme of life with more fixed lines. He disdained nothing that could advance him in knowledge and intellectual strength : and I have often heard him say that the great marvels of science, such as were shown us in the lectures to working men that we attended, stirred his soul to religious feeling just like the passion of prayer. And what he knew and valued for himself, that he was eager to impart to others. And it was this which made him begin his " night school," where he got together all who would come, and tried to interest them in some of the more taking " fairy tales of science," as well as to teach them a few homely truths in the way of cleanliness, health, good cooking, and the like ; with interludes, so to speak, of lessons in morality; winding up with a few simple prayers and an attempt to make his hearers feel the Presence and the Power of God. All came to this meeting who would ; thieves and drunkards, lost women and gutter-children—no matter who : there was a kindly welcome for all ; no preaching at them for their sins ; no expression of spiritual or moral superiority, but just the great loving equality which does the degraded so much good, and gives them, if only for a moment, a flash of natural self-respect and the glorious sense of inclusion and brotherhood. So that you see his life was not a meagre one ; and while he blessed others so far as his power went, he grew daily riper in his own thoughts, and fuller of knowledge, and more clear as to what he meant.

We were very poor all this time : that of course we understood we must be. We were accustomed to it, and would have been more embarrassed with a lot of surplus money to spend, if we had had to spend it on ourselves, than we were to make the best of the little we possessed. But we did look to live like decent men, and not like savages. And we desired the same for our order. Yet how was that possible in the conditions in which we found ourselves? And we were only two out of thousands.

We lodged in a stifling court, Church-court, where every room was filled as if cubic inches were gold, as indeed they are to London house-owners, if human life is but dross. Children swarmed like rabbits in every house, and died like sheep with the rot. It was sore to see them, poor little, pale, stunted, half-naked creatures, playing about the foul uncleansed pavement of the court, from the reeking gutter of which they picked up apple-parings, potato-peelings, fish-heads, and the like, which I have seen them many a time wipe on their rags and eat. "The bronchitis" it was called that sent so many of them to the hospital and the graveyard, but the real word was poverty : poverty in everything ; in food, in clothing, in care, in lodging. It made one's heart ache to see them—them and their parents too : the hopeless misery of their lives and the moral degradation following. And it made one think with deep amazement of what the wisdom of that nation could be which leaves its riches to rot in the gutter for want of looking after and tending; not to speak of the religion, which contents itself with building churches, and endowing foreign and colonial bishoprics, while its own immortal souls perish for lack of the Bread of Life squandered in baskets full on the altars to Baal ! Where to find the issue ? How to fill up the great chasm between the rich and the poor, the virtuous and the vicious, the learned and the ignorant, the civilised and the brutish?

"There is only one way out of it," said a noted M.P. to Joshua one day, a great political economist and a strict Malthusian: "abstinence; if you wish to see the poor raised you must lighten the labour market by bringing fewer labourers into it. That is the first necessity. Leave off having children, live frugally, and put by money, and as many of you can, emigrate."

"Is this not omitting one important factor from your calculations, sir?" said Joshua.

"What do you mean?" asked Mr. ——.

"Merely the human nature there is in humanity," said Joshua. "Do you think the poor have no instincts? Is not a wife or a husband, a home where there are little children, sometimes a day's pleasure, and the old family ties of father and mother and brothers and sisters—are not all these as dear to them as to the rich? Why should they be required to forego these that the rich may not be called upon to share?"

"Would you destroy the existing order of society?" said the M.P. sternly.

"Destroy it? aye! root and branch, if need be! In no civilised community—not to speak of a Christian one, if Christianity meant anything—ought there to be such places as Belgrave-square and Church-court. Keep your Belgrave-square by all means, but let the Church-courts be made at least wholesome and decent."

"You have the remedy in your own hands," said the M.P. "So long as you will marry on nothing, spend all you get, and breed paupers, paupers you must remain, wallowing in filth and wretchedness. The whole question is as much a matter of exact science as any other mathematical problem; and you are to blame, Davidson, that you do not abandon your foolish rant about Christian charity and human rights, and apply yourself to the only way out of the difficulty—the science of Political Economy."

Joshua smiled sadly. "Political Economy is not quite human enough for us, sir," he said. "It rests too on the basis of these very existing conditions of society that I do not care for; I would rather see something more radical, going straight to the root of the evil."

"You are an enthusiast," said the M. P. coldly. "I tell you again, Political Economy does go to the root of the evil; and the only thing that does."

"Then Christianity is wrong," said Joshua.

And the M.P. was silent. He had never confessed himself on the subject of religion, and never would. Not his most intimate friends knew what he believed or what he did not believe. All that the world saw was that he went to church, made the orthodox bow at the Name in the Creed, and wrote books and pamphlets full of anti-Christian, hard-headed doctrines, without ever once alluding to religious dogma. When he was called an infidel by his foes he hit out savagely, and said, "Prove it." And no man could: only every man felt that his whole teaching, from first to last, was absolutely devoid of all Christian feeling; that pity, charity, warmth, and love were as far from him as heaven is from the earth; and that he squared the accounts of humanity with the most sublime unconsciousness that such disturbing elements as passions or the sentiment of rights existed to upset his sums and prove his sociology for the present at least imperfect.

And the result of the conversation was, that Mr. ——, the M.P., who is a worthy man, upright and honourable, but practically one-sided because so utterly undisturbed by weakness or passions of any kind, and therefore unable to allow for them in another, denounced Joshua as a mischievous agitator and an ignorant fanatic, and warned those of us whom he knew to beware of him. Yet Mr. —— was as hearty as Joshua himself in his desire to see the regeneration of the working class: but as Joshua said, and I thought said well too; " He advocates our making ourselves so slender that we can slip through our bands and fetters, while I hold that we should make ourselves strong enough to force those who hold the fastenings to loosen them. We both mean the same thing in the end, liberty and social advancement; but we differ as to the means."

Our court was one of just ordinary moral character, neither strictly respectable nor the reverse. We had all sorts; from the man who would harbour a pal in trouble and stow away swag not honestly come by till the police scent grew cold, to the decent workman doing his best to be respectable, and to keep his girls pure and his boys honest; from the hard working-woman slaving night and day to make her two poor ends meet, to the idle slattern who was drunk

half her time, and begged in the streets the
other half; from the fond mother with her
pretty pride in Sunday frocks or bits of
coloured bows, to the husbandless wench
whose half-starved children, as naked as
crows and nearly as black, were knocked
about as if they were street dogs, and on the
highway to the gallows through neglect;
from the virtuous spinster proud of her character and intolerant of looseness, to the poor
flaunting girl who got her living in the
streets, leastwise eked out her scanty wages
from slopwork and the like by prostitution,
more or less avowed.

One of these girls lived just opposite
to us. Her name was Mary Prinsep.
We had seen her at a music-hall we went
to by times: for Joshua was not one
of those prudes who are afraid of ap-

pearances, and as he wanted to learn the world on all sides he went to all sorts of places and talked to all sorts of people—to these poor girls, as well as to any one else, and just as he would to any one else ; seeking to know the causes of things, and why they went on to the streets, and if they would keep out of them if they could, and so on.

Any one who knows anything about us working men as we are and not by fancy portraits, knows the profound contempt, and more, in which as a class we hold the professed prostitute, or the woman of our own homes who lets herself be seduced by a gentleman. A base child—nay, more than one, and by different fathers too—if by men of our own class is not so unpardonable an offence. We think it a pity, of course, and we would rather not have it happen to our daughters and sisters; but we get over it; and the women not unfrequently marry, and marry well, when the thing has blown by a little. But the poor, painted, bedizened wreck of womanhood who goes about the streets at the West-end, and sells herself to club-gentlemen and the like, is of all things that of which we have the most abhorrence. I don't pretend to explain it, and very likely it is only a matter of class jealousy when all is said and done; but I mention it as a kind of introduction to what I have to say of Mary Prinsep. I want it to be seen that it was no indifferentism to her trade which actuated Joshua; but, on the contrary, that it was the large and generous humanity in him which made him able to accept even a street-walker as his sister and his friend.

Mary was very young and very ignorant. She had been brought up any how, and had been neglected and untaught from the beginning. There was no romantic history attached to her. She was no " soiled dove " whose feathers had once been white and shining; she was the daughter of a dram-drinking charwoman, sent out to mind children when quite a child herself, brought up to no trade, and knowing nothing now but the streets and the music-halls. But she had so much to the good, that she did not drink—at least not much—they all drink some; and she had never been in trouble or locked up. She was merely one of the abandoned—abandoned by society from her birth, and left to sink or swim in the foul streams of the metropolis as she best could. She had been picked up by a gentleman a few years ago when she was about fifteen; and he had taught her a good deal both of refinement and womanly ways. She had been grateful to him at the time, but she scarcely loved him. He was older than herself; in fact, an old man comparatively; married, with grown-up daughters and sons, a churchwarden, and a fine Christian gentleman living out at Bayswater in the very odour of class respectability. But he had an eye for pretty girls; and he had placed Mary in a little house at Bow, where, as I said, she had learned some things that were useful to her, being a girl of great natural quickness, and, if she had had fair play, of refined taste and good disposition. In time he got tired of her. Such men always do: for what was there in an ignorant girl like that to keep him when he had had enough of

her beauty? So, making her a handsome present—oh! he behaved to her quite handsomely!—he parted with her, and Mary had
to turn out into the streets with a ruined
character and a taste for good living. She
had learned however, during her two or three
years of "protection," to keep herself and
her place tidy, and to do needlework after a
fashion, but not sufficiently well to keep her.
Twelve hours a day of slop-work would not
feed, clothe, and lodge her; flower-selling
would not; but her youth and good looks
would. So she sold them, as all she had to
sell; and got bread of the devil's baking because she could not get it any way else.

It was a bad life; and she felt it was. And
it was a hard life too. Those who see these
girls only in their show-hours, dressed in the
height of the fashion and queening it at

night-houses and the like, have no idea of
the wretchedness of the reality for the poorer
kind; for there are classes even here. No
wonder they take to drink, poor souls, suffering as they do—merciful Heaven, how
they do suffer! And how some of them
loathe their lives as they go on, and go
down, and wish they had died before they
took up the trade! Not that I say for
an instant they go moaning about in eternal
agonies of remorse or horror—human nature does not live at such high pressure; but
a lot of them do hate their business never-
theless, when the drink is not in them and
their vanity is not flattered.

But—virtuous women will start at this—
they look on themselves, like all the poor, as
martyrs to society. They think that, as
men and things are, they must be; that they

make the virtuous wife, the chaste maiden, possible. In their blind way they are vaguely conscious that the root of this fine flower of western civilisation, the rich monogamous Christian home, is planted in the filth of prostitution, and that to them is owing the "self-restraint," so much admired in gentlemen who do not marry until they can afford to have a family, and so often offered as an example to us working men who love honestly one of our own sort, and do not as a rule go among these girls. And the more thoughtful of them, conscious of their economic uses, resent the opprobrium dealt out to them, and pity themselves angrily as victims rather than criminals, the scapegoats not the polluters of society.

To be sure, they do not fret at the scorn of the great ladies whom they help to keep virtuous, for they have their compensations. Fine ladies think that because they would not brush skirts with a prostitute, therefore no one will, and that all life shows them the same aspect of repulsion and horror. It is nothing of the kind. Decent women of the poorer class, consort with them, if not cordially yet humanely; then they have friends of their own sort, and many of them; and we know that a multitude of evil doers makes the evil done seem light to each. The gentlemen who go with them are often kind and playful, and no more brutal than most men are to most women outside the artificial restraints of society. Sometimes, of course, they are vile enough; but these are the men who would be brutal to their own lady-wives and daughters. So that the poor Girls, as they call themselves, are not quite shut out from all human sympathy like the lepers of old — though indeed the circle is terribly narrowed! And though many of them have fits of self-loathing and regret, others take matters more coolly, and look on their profession as a legitimate trade, as lawful as a publican's who sells the gin that robs a man's family of bread, and makes him perhaps a murderer as well as a madman.

Mary Prinsep was what the world calls lost—a bad girl—a castaway—but she might have been a saint for the natural virtue that was in her. I have reason to speak well of her, for to her we owe the life of Joshua.

Soon after we came to know her, Joshua fell ill in our wretched lodgings where we lived and did for ourselves. He did not like to go to the hospital, nor did I like it for him. We both had a strong feeling against accepting the charity of society; so I said he should not go, and that I would work harder for him and myself too. But by my harder work — overtime, and the like — I was obliged to leave him for twelve hours and more at a stretch; and Mary Prinsep, whose "friend" had just left her to go into a west-end "dress-house," poor wench! came over and nursed him, and kept him alive.

She it was who made up the fire, cooked his broths and messes, gave him his medicine, washed his clothes, and kept him clean and comfortable. And when I came home from work, and found her there, with everything arranged so nicely and as only a woman can—Joshua's bed made and him settled for the night, and my own supper ready, and hot water for cleaning

myself—for we had but one room between
us—as one of the great family of the frail,
the suffering, I could not feel anything like
virtuous horror of her. She was our sister—
our sister of sorrow, of poverty, of affliction.

Gladly would Joshua have lifted her out
of her life into something purer and nobler.
He was so poor himself with all he did and
gave away, he had much ado to live on the
leavings ; and as for marrying, that was as
unlikely as murder! So that he could
neither put her into any way of business
independently, nor give her a home that the
world would not misjudge. We did what
we could, however. I say *we* intentionally,
as it makes the whole thing clear to those
who are candid enough not to wilfully mis-
understand. We helped her all we could,
and she helped us. We worked for her

food, while she gave us her time and did our chores. And so in this way we made it unnecessary for her to continue her sad trade.

This got us the name of associating with bad women; for it was said that we lived partly on her earnings; and made us to be shyly looked on by our shopmates. But Joshua's mind was set to do the thing that is right; and what men said against him, not understanding facts or motives, hurt him no more than that dogs should bark at shadows. That which is, not that which seems, nor what folks choose to say, was what he lived for; and Mary Prinsep was only a text and an occasion, like others.

And even when, one day, the men fairly hooted him down and hustled him into the street, and me along with him, because when he was chaffed savagely about "his girl" he answered them mildly enough; "Mates, did our great Master receive Mary Magdalene and all sinners, or did He not? And if He did—as you may find for your-selves—am *I* too pure to help them?"—he only said to me, wiping the mud from his torn coat; "You are not afraid, John? You'll go on the right way, whatever comes of it?"—and not a word even of impatience against those who had misused us, calling us "canters," "white-livered hypocrites," and worse words still. No, I was not afraid, I said. I would stand shoulder to shoulder with him through it all; and where he led, there would I follow, if we sunk up to our very necks in the slough of the world's reproach. And we were not far off.

CHAPTER VI.

AMONG the rest of the doubtful characters
with which our court abounded, was one Joe
Traill, who had been in prison many a time
for petty larceny and the like, but who, the
last time he was had up, was convicted of
burglary. However, he was out now on a
ticket-of-leave, and fast going the way to
get it cancelled, with a new score to the
back of it. Respectability and the police
were bent on elbowing poor Joe into the mire,
which was only too much his natural ele-
ment. He had been crotch deep in the mud
from the earliest; a gutter child, in whose

very blood ran the hereditary taint; a thief, the son of thieves, the grandson of thieves; a thing of mud from head to heel, inside and out; dirty, dissipated, shiftless, and with no more moral principle in him than he had of education. His only morality indeed, was his cleverness in being able to break the law without being found out; and when he was most down on his luck, he was disposed to think most meanly of himself.

He was one of those who stink in the nostrils of cleanly, civilised society, and who are its shame and secret sore. And cleanly, civilised society, not being able to make a good job of him as he stood, thrust him out of its sight, and tried to forget him behind the prison grating. There was no place for Joe in this great world of ours. There was no work for him to do, because he could do none requiring any of the deftness got by practice; and if by chance he got a job anywhere, he lost it mysteriously in a day or so; and, double as he might, he found the dogs of detection too sharp for him.

So he said to Joshua one night in his blithe way---poor Joe! he had not fibre enough in him to take even his misfortunes seriously!—that there was nothing for him but the old line along with his pals, making a running fight of it, now up now down, as his luck went.

"We'll see if something better won't turn up," said Joshua. "Burglary's a bad trade, Joe."

"Only one I've got at my fingers' ends, governor," laughed the thief; "and starvation is a worse go than quod."

"Well, till you've learned a better, share

with us," said Joshua. "If we have no widow's cruse——" "Blowed if I know what that means!" put in Joe, " —we have what does as well," continued Joshua; "and it's better for four to go short than for one to be rationed at the hulks."

So now our little home circle was increased by one more; and we had added a burglar to the prostitute.

"It is what Christ would have done," said Joshua, when he was remonstrated with. "He lived among the lepers whom no man would touch, and whose very presence was pollution. But he healed some among them; and so will I these."

But the police did not see it. They do not understand practical Christianity in Scotland-yard, save as a generous kind of fad or pastime in a swell with more money

than brains, and a lot of idle time on his
hands. And then they laugh at it behind
backs, and ridicule him for being green.
But when it came to a poor journeyman carpenter housing a jail-bird, and consorting
with bad characters daily, they had but one
conclusion to come to—the carpenter was
no better than his company. Wherefore,
" from information received," Joshua and I,
who had long been looked on askance by
our mates as I said, were called up before
the master, and had our dismissal from the
shop. His other men, he said, objected to
us ; and, by the Lord, from all he had been
told he did not wonder at it ! And he
gave us a caution—kindly meant, if harshly
said—not to keep such company as we did,
if we wanted to be respected by master or
mate and to remember that " birds of a

feather flock together," and if we chose such birds as he was told we did, we could look for nothing else than to be classed along with them. On which he paid us our week's wages, and we found ourselves next thing to penniless in the wilds of London.

But Joshua was undisturbed. He told both Joe and Mary, on the evening we were discharged, that he would not forsake them come what might. It should still be share and share alike; only let them be of good courage and a clean conscience, and things would go well. How, nobody knew; but this is what he said, and promised.

And Mary, looking up into his face with a look that made her like an angel—for indeed she was a pretty girl!—said, "If I have to starve, Joshua, I'll never go back to the streets again!" and poor Joe, first laughing, and then sobbing like a woman, said, "You'd have done better to have left me to my little game, governor! I've brought you bad luck, you see; and I'm no good, you see, when you've done your best!"

"Don't carry on like that, Joe," said Joshua. "I shall have done something if I save you both: and I will."

I could not help thinking that this "I will," said with such manly courage, such deep religious firmness, was a greater trial of faith than the boyish exaltation in the Rocky Valley so many years ago; and that to save from the streets a girl who was not able to do anything else that the world wants, and to put honesty and a clean name into such a poor conscienceless waif as Joe, were greater deeds than to cause a stone to move out of its place in the Name of the Lord.

And all of us, his old Cornish friends who had come up to be near him, and some new friends he had made in London, swore we would never desert him, but would stand by him to the last. For we looked that he should do something in his day, as I said before—something to advance the world, and towards the solution of the great questions perplexing society at this moment. True, we were a poor, moneyless lot—all working men, no science among us, no political power, no social status, no political-economy knowledge of the right sort; a handful of enthusiasts set out to realise Christ at one time by faith, and now by works. But we had a soul among us—a leader in whom we believed; and we trusted in ourselves. And one by one we all got to work again some-how, and floated in the shallow but sufficient water to which we were accustomed. But it was a hard time; and, bit by bit, every-thing we possessed passed over the pawn-broker's counter, even to our tools. And when they went, it seemed as if all hope had gone.

But when we were at the worst, and things looked as though they had given over all thought of mending—for we were getting whersh and weak for want of food—Joshua received a letter enclosing a five-pound note, "from a friend." We never knew where it came from, and there was no clue by which we could guess. It was very certain that neither had Mary earned it in the old way, nor had Joe stolen it; but who sent it re-mained for ever a mystery. I always thought that Mary had had a hand in it, and I think so to this day. I believe, though I don't know, that she borrowed it of an artist to whom she went to sit for a model; for she did not make any secret of this; and that she paid it back honestly when we were in funds again. However that might be, it came at the very nick of time; and immediately after, both Joshua and I got the offer of a job at Messrs. —— in Curtain-road, which we could not have accepted had we not had money wherewith to take our tools out of pawn It was a sharp pinch while it lasted, but, God be praised, it passed without doing real harm to any one. And Joe and Mary still bided with us.

By this time Joshua's strange doings in Church-court had got known to some of the gentlemen who practise philanthropy. His night-school for those who would learn either prayer or secular knowledge of him—his charity dinners, when he could get enough money together to give them—his goodness to the children, to the lost, to the starving—all this had got wind; and just as he wanted help most, the news of his doings brought him the famous Mr. C. anxious to know how a man like him could carry on charities, apparently on nothing, which cost himself a large income to keep up.

He was a good man, this Mr. C.; up to his lights, none better; but his lights were few and feeble, and he drew a line hard and fast where Joshua did not. His line was respectability. He distinctly refused to aid those who were hopeless paupers, or those of bad repute. He would help respectable poverty, and help it substantially though always

afraid of overdoing it and inducing a habit
of reliance on extraneous aid ; but beasted,
shiftless, drunken poverty—poverty that
lied and whined and drank gin and got
relief from half-a-dozen charities at once—
poverty that was its own cause and that
never stirred a hand to help itself—for
this he had no pity, and to it gave no
help.

" To encourage pauperism" and "to offer
a premium for vice " were the two things of
which he was most afraid in his dealings
with the poor; but he held out a helping
hand gladly enough to the " deserving " and
the " respectable " poor, and he was a warm
patron of reformatories, refuges for soiled
doves, and the like half-punitive places of
retreat for sinful flesh, where they might
repent of their evil past, and be made fit to

take up a lowly place among the respectable
members of society once more ;—but always,
in a sense, a place of humiliation and peni-
tent degradation.

As he came along at this time, and was
handy, and as Mary's friend, the artist, had
gone to Italy for some months, and she had
no other patron of the like kind, so was out
of work as one may say, to him Joshua told
the whole story of both her and Joe Traill ;
also how he had kept them in the best way
he could from the evil to which society had
driven them in former days : he did not add
the rider of how society had revenged itself
on him as on them, and cast us all out in
company.   But now, he said, he was de-
sirous of placing them both where their
temptation would be towards honesty;
where it would be better for them to be

honest, and where falling back would plunge them into misery as well as shame.

Mr. C. listened attentively. He was evidently touched by the high spirit of the man, but he greatly questioned the wisdom of his ways. For Joe, he said, he scarcely knew what to propose. He shrank from committing himself to the patronage of a convicted thief, who was not a boy to be sent to a reformatory and disciplined into good ways. It was out of his line altogether, and he had no machinery at hand for him. Had he been a broken-down, sober, honest, and industrious chap, who had failed through sickness or any blameless misfortune, he would then have given him a lift willingly; but a man who had slipped into the dark ways of crime, who had got into houses at dead of night with a crowbar and a jemmy—he shook his head, and said he did not like to have anything to do with him. It was offering a premium to vice to take trouble to place this unsatisfactory waif and stray, when hundreds of honest men, who had never gone wrong, were perishing for want of aid.

"As for that," said Joshua, "I ask nothing, whether this man sinned or his parents; or neither. He is in want; and, to my way of thinking, his need is his claim, not his respectability."

Mr. C. looked dubious. "We must draw a line," he said.

"Christ drew it at the Pharisee," answered Joshua simply.

"To make no difference between vice and virtue—to treat the one as tenderly as the other—would soon be to obliterate all difference between them in minds as well as in practice," said Mr. C.

"And what, then, do we say to the parable of the men who worked unequally, and who got the same wages at the end?" said Joshua.

"My good fellow," cried Mr. C. a little impatiently, "it would be perfectly impossible to try and live strictly after the Bible. 'Counsels of perfection' are all very well, but they are impracticable for the world as it is."

"I have to find that out yet," said Joshua. "Then you will not help me with poor Joe?"

"Do not say I will not—I cannot," said Mr. C. "How can I ask my poor, honest pensioners, or my respectable workmen, to receive a convicted thief among them?"

"'And forgive us our trespasses, as we

forgive them that trespass against us.'
Does that mean only petty, personal affronts,
sir, or does it mean trespass against our
patience, our hope, our faith, our principles?
Does it not mean the everlasting Love,
whether we call it charity or humanity, by
which we would raise the fallen and help
the weak?"

"As for that," retorted Mr. C., "there are
texts enough against consorting with evil.
You cannot touch pitch, Mr. Davidson, without being defiled."

"Christ lodged in the house of Simon the
leper. Mary Magdalene loved Him, and He
her. I want no other example, sir. What
the Master did, His followers and disciples
may imitate!"

"You are an enthusiast," said Mr. C.
just as the M.P. had said before him, and

both meant that enthusiasm was ridiculous;
"and some day these fine theories of yours
will come to a cruel downfall. You will be
harbouring some ruffian who will turn
against you, and perhaps cut your throat for
your pains. I tell you I know these people
—they are incorrigible."

"Then what would you do with them,
Mr. C.?"

"You can do nothing with them!" he
answered.

"But they cannot be let to starve," said
Joshua earnestly.

"I do not see that it is any one's duty to
feed them, when they will not feed themselves save by vice and crime," answered
the philanthropist. "I would make all
rogues, male and female, show some tangible signs of repentance and good living

before I would help them or countenance them in any way. Believe me, your universal charity is the most disastrous line you could adopt."

"Then Christ was wrong," said Joshua : "and so we have come round to our starting-point again. So this is decided—you will not give Joe Traill a trial ? "

"No ; I would rather not have anything to do with him," said Mr. C., who had talked himself cross and determined. "I should never be easy with the fellow. I have no fancy for burglars, and I don't believe in their reformation. All my men are picked men ; not a loose character among them. I could not ask them to admit a convicted thief as one of them ; and if I did, my own influence over them would be gone. It is because they know I

K

would never pardon the smallest dereliction of duty that I keep them up to the mark : with what face then could I place among them such an unsatisfactory companion as your *protégé?* The thing would be impossible! With the woman perhaps I can do something. If she is young, she cannot be wholly hardened, and I could get her into the —— Street Reformatory."

"No," said Joshua, "I will not consent to her going into a reformatory. It is not that she needs. In a reformatory she will be continually reminded of what I want her to forget. She would be made morbid by incessant thought about herself; taught to say penitential psalms when she should be set to learn some skilled employment that would be of use to her in the future. I wish her to be kept virtuous through self-respect,

and by being placed beyond the need of going
back to such a life. I do not want her to
be weakened by a self-torturing contrition
for the past, or terrified at the prospect of
eternal damnation for the future. I want
her to be lifted up, not cast down."

"You surely do not make light of repentance!" cried Mr. C. warmly. "What
other assurance have we that she will not
fail again?"

"The best assurance, sir, will be to teach
her self-respect and the means of gaining an
honest living," said Joshua.

"You are a rank materialist, Davidson!" said Mr. C. "I cannot stand your
referring sin to mere social conditions. Are
there no such things as sins in high places?
Poverty and ignorance are not the only
roots of human wickedness!"

"About the strongest though," Joshua answered.

"And the sins of luxury——"

"Make Mary Prinsep and her class," interrupted Joshua. "See here, sir, what are you asked to do?—to repair, in a very small way, the evil done by society. You represent society at this moment, and you are asked to undo a portion of your own bad work."

"Pshaw!" said Mr. C. "*I* have not made Mary bad!"

He was an individual kind of man, and never saw beyond his own point.

"Well," he then said, "I will do what I can for the young woman. My wife wants an under-servant; I will put the case to her; but I rely on you," he added, old habits of thought coming back to steady him in this sudden taking-off of his feet, as it were; "I rely on you that I am dealing with a woman substantially repentant, and so far purified; and that she will not corrupt the rest. For it is a dangerous experiment at the best."

"She is good enough for any one to trust and to love," said Joshua warmly; and Mr. C. looked at him with a sharp, suspicious glance that quite changed his face. "And I thank you heartily," Joshua went on to say, unconscious that he had caused the slightest discomfort in the gentleman's mind; "you have done a good work to-day — a work of brotherhood with Christ."

"I trust I am not doing wrong," said Mr. C. doubtfully; "but it is against my principles, you know. I cannot help feeling that I am rewarding a woman, because she has lived a life of infamy, with a position which hundreds of virtuous girls would be rejoiced to fill."

"If your economic conscience troubles you, sir, lay it at rest by the answer our Lord made to Himself, when He asked the Canaanitish woman if it were meet to cast the children's bread to dogs."

"For all that, I cannot think it a duty to reward vice," persisted Mr. C. "And in doing what I am doing now, I wish it to be distinctly understood that it is at your instance."

"Which means that you refuse the responsibility?"

"It does."

"So be it, sir. I accept it."

"That will not help me much if the thing

turns out ill," said Mr. C. in a discomposed voice.

"Oh, sir, have faith in human nature!" said Joshua earnestly—so earnestly that I believe the tears were in his eyes: they were in his voice.

"It is because I know human nature that I have so little faith in it," said Mr. C. "Every one wants the help of strict moral principle to enable him to steer clear of the temptations so sure to beset him, and these fallen brothers and sisters are but leaky vessels at the best. If human nature was the grand thing you say it is, Mr. Davidson, of what need the coming of Christ? You are a Christian."

"And it is because Christ lived that I believe in humanity," said Joshua.

On which, Mr. C. saying with a smile,

"There is no doing anything with you, Mr. Davidson ; you are as unconvinceable as a woman," shook hands with him kindly enough, and left.

A day or two after this he came again, with many kind words, much regret and I doubt not genuine, but—his wife was as afraid of our poor Mary as he had been of Joe Traill, and refused to take her into her house. If the other servants should ever know; if Mary had imposed on Joshua, and was really of no good ; if she should corrupt the younger ones ; and then the repute of their house—the duty they owed their neighbours to keep up a stainless appearance. No, there could be no home for her there ; but the lady sent a note, full of that half-censorious advice a virtuous woman knows so well how to administer to her fallen sisters — a parcel of tracts (Mary could not read), and a renewal of her husband's offer to get her in the —— Street Reformatory. After which perhaps some kind Christian person would be found to take her, she said, endorsed as she would then be by the Lady Superintendent of the establishment. For without casting any slur on Mr. Davidson, she went on to say, the voucher of only a young man was not quite satisfactory to a mistress who cared for the honour of her house. And perhaps she was right. But then Joshua was not like other young men; only she did not know this; and Christians think it no sin to suspect all manner of evil of each other, unless they know for certain it does not exist.

Well, it was a disappointment; but

Joshua was not a man to be cast down for one blow or a dozen; so he set to work to find some one who would take her, knowing her past life; and at last lighted on a good, tender-hearted, but timid woman, who received her in full faith so far as the girl herself was concerned, but on the express condition that no one should ever know what she had been, and that there was to be no kind of communication between her and ourselves, or any of her old Church-court friends. To these terms Joshua advised her to submit; so with many tears poor Mary went away to take the place of kitchen-maid in a family living at a little distance from London, where, as the lady said, she had a chance now of redeeming herself, and a new start given her altogether.

"And if I do well, Joshua, you will be

pleased with me?" she said as she was bidding us good-by.

"More than pleased, Mary," he said. "You know that I trust you, and that we both love you—John here as well as I."

Mary's face was as white as the frill round her neck. "Joshua!" she said, looking up at him, "give me one kiss before I go ; it will help me."

Joshua bent his noble head and kissed her tenderly.

"God be with you, sister!" he said, and his voice a little failed him.

"And I will say the prayer you taught me, Joshua, regularly morning and evening when I ain't too sleepy," said Mary simply. "And you will pray for me too ?"

"As I do ever, my girl," said Joshua: "and I believe that God hears us!"

"Then He will hear me!" said Mary with a kindling face; "and I'll pray harder nor ever for the thing I want!"

Poor Mary! prayer was naught but a "charm" to her as yet. She had never heard one, never offered one, till Joshua taught her the Lord's Prayer, with a childish hymn and a childish "God bless all I love" at the end; and she repeated what she had been taught as a young child might; believing that it did good because she had been told so by one she loved and trusted, but realising nothing more. Or if she realised anything, it was that she prayed to Joshua, grown very great and strong, and a long way off.

CHAPTER VII.

Joshua's life of work and endeavour brought with it no reward of praise or popularity. It suffered the fate of all unsectarianism, and made him to be as one man in the midst of foes. Had he been a converted sinner like Ned Wright, preaching the doctrine of the Atonement, and Purification by the blood of Jesus, he would have had all the evangelical force at his back, pivoted as they are on the same hub, whatever their special denomination. Had he been a Ritualist, working under organised authority, he would have then been a pipe, so

to speak, through which flowed the power of
the Church; and this much more had he
been a Roman Catholic, and of any Order.
Had he been a Unitarian, a stickler for respectability and that the poor he relieved
should be deserving, like Mr. C. and the
charity-organisation people; or a Political
Economist, giving lectures on the law of
supply and demand, and the immorality of
large families; had he belonged to any body
whatsoever, he would have been supported.
But, as he was—a man working on the
Christ plan, and that alone; dealing with
Humanity by pity and love and tolerance
—he was as a stranger and an alien.

The whole force of home missionaries of
every denomination discountenanced him as
an infidel, unsound, irregular; and in whatsoever they disagreed among themselves,

they all agreed in their ill estimate of him. The police were suspicious of him, and set him down as a doubtful character who harboured criminals; and the very people to whom he gave himself—accustomed as they were to be scouted by every man and woman pretending to clean hands and a pure life, or, at the best, to be preached at and urged to remorse -- misdoubted him. The absence of abhorrence in his dealings with them looked to some like a trap, to others like encouragement. And yet they could scarcely think that!—with all his endeavours to put them into a better way of life, and to lift them out of the necessity of crime by giving them the alternative of honesty made possible, because giving them work sufficient for their daily wants.

But he soon began to see that the utmost

he, or a dozen such as he, could do, was only palliative and temporary. He might save one out of a thousand, and he would do well if he did that ; but what is one out of a thousand cleansed and set in a safe place, to the nine hundred and ninety-nine left in their filth at the bottom of the abyss ? Things have gone too far in England now for private charities to be of much use. What is wanted is a thorough reorganisation of society, so that the distribution of wealth and knowledge shall not be so partial as it is. And this the working classes must get for themselves by combination.

So Joshua turned to class-organisation as something more hopeful than private charity. But do not let me be misunderstood : he gave up nothing of his own personal doings among the poor, and never wearied nor relaxed. If he looked to organisation as the framework, he did not disdain charity as the enrichment, in the plan of social amelioration.

When the International Working Men's Association was formed, he joined it as one of its first members; indeed he mainly helped to establish it. It had been one of his articles of belief long before any one else had spoken, that the time had passed for distinct and exclusive nationalities; and that if working men would free themselves from the fetters in which capital and caste have bound them, it must be by their own class-fraternisation all over the world. If labour is to make its own terms with capital, it must be by the coercive strength of the labourer. To wait for the free gift of the capitalist, through his recognition of human duties, as some among the Comtists urge, would be to wait for the millennium. Yet the International represented no class enmity with him. He had no dream of barricades and high places taken by assault. It was to him, as to his other English brethren, an organisation to strengthen the hands of the labourer everywhere, but not to plunge society into a bloody war. It was a means of class-advancement by peaceable and noble efforts, not of universal destruction by violent or ignoble ones.

The middle classes laugh at the artisan's desire to rise in the world, and speak of his close combinations as traitorous and rebellious to the existing order of things. Some think it an irreligious contempt of a caste-Providence; forgetting that their own order was made by the same spirit of determination, and that the recognition of the merchant class, and its reception on anything like terms of equality, was forced from the nobles by men who had at heart the great truth of human equality and human rights; at least, down to that part of the social page where their own names stood. Below that paragraph where the artisan, the *prolétaire*, is to be found, society has as yet drawn a line not to be overpassed. Demand rights and recognition for working men, and even the Liberal press gives forth an uncertain sound, and the bugbear of "Jack Cade" scares such stout hearts as the *Pall Mall* and the *Spectator*. Even they, kings of liberal thought as they are in so many ways, will not see that the modern artisan stands in the same relation to capital as that in which the ancient serf stood to the land. The serf tilled the land, which was his master's, for his master. If he could get for himself a living about as good as that of the hogs he forested, he had all that was considered necessary for a serf. And the artisan represents the serf of olden days, while capital is the foretime baron. The baron gave his villein disdainful leave to live because his life was so far requisite to his own needs; but individually he had neither rights nor value. So the capitalist. He gives his workmen only enough to keep them in efficient working order—or not that, if the labour market is so thronged that he can replace without trouble those who fall out. His "hands" are the mere parts of his machinery. The sum of them work to a certain result; but he is indifferent whether the work is done with sorrow and insuffi-

ziency to the individual or not. His sole
business is to see that the sum get through
their labours creditably—to the firm. It is
good that the work of the world should be
done at all costs, even by compulsory labour
if need be ; but it is better that it should be
done by men regarded as men, individual,
and having inalienable rights, rather than as
so many portions of a vitalised mechanism.
And a fair and proportionate share in the
profits of the business is part of the rights
of the labourer.

I am speaking now as if of myself; but I
am only repeating what I have heard my
friend say scores of times.

Of course Joshua was an earnest Republican. Who that thinks for himself can
fail to be one ? Not that he would have
put aside the reigning sovereign by force,

but he held that the times were ripening for the old monarchical symbol and aristocratic exclusiveness to disappear now that the reality had gone; and that the Republic would come about of itself, thanks, in great part, to the monarch who has shown the people that royalty can be dispensed with and yet things go none the worse for the withdrawal, and to the aristocracy which has abandoned its old traditions of blood and birth, and has sold so many of its blue ribands to money. But he was not a Republican of the kind to rave and vilify, and accuse all the higher classes of wilful misdoing, of vice and selfishness, and what not. He never abused anybody, but judged things by their merits, and gave to the professors of any doctrine, no matter what, at least the credit of sincerity. By which he made many enemies, and was constantly accused of lukewarmness to the cause, and of looking two ways at once.

"You cannot beat me off my point," he used to say, when he had put into an uproar a little inner and anonymous society which some few of us had formed together, by vindicating some man whose measures he also had attacked. "I say that we do our cause harm, and degrade ourselves, by all these childish personalities. What we have to do is, to defend our own principles, and show the fallacy or the evil of our opponents'; but we must fight fair, and give that credit for honesty of purpose which we demand for ourselves. If we are thieves and brigands to the governing classes, and they are thieves and brigands to us, what kind of understanding can we ever come to together?"

But L., one of those fanatical men who cannot accept the doctrine of an opponent's virtue, and whose zeal takes the form of the wildest abuse on all who differ from him, got up and denounced Joshua as an "inherent traitor," and advised his expulsion from the society. And more than one of the council looked grave, and as if they were giving their minds to it, had not Félix Pyat risen, and given his opinion so forcibly that the malcontents were silenced. Even the thin-voiced little man who had denounced Joshua, and whose ambition was to be regarded as the Robespierre of the society—incorruptible, and not to be moved by fear or favour—even he had to give in. For Félix was our giant; and Félix loved Joshua.

This was at the time when he was over

here as an exile, chiefly reading at the
British Museum, and when he gained the
love and admiration of all who knew him
by the dignity, the devotion, the earnestness
of his life. I mention this somewhat by
the way, as my feeble protest against the
terms in which it is the fashion to speak of
one of the finest fellows that ever lived—as
fine in his own way as Delescluze, our martyr,
—and by those who ought to know better;
and who do know better; but who think it
politic to swim with the stream, and to
curse those whom fortune has not blessed.

From his position in the International,
and in other political societies—which abound
among the working men more than the care-
less upper ten have the least idea of—
Joshua was thrown into intimate relations
with a great many men, more or less no·

torious. He saw all sorts—the frothy ranter whose motive power was vanity; the reckless agitator whose conscience was obscured, and, so long as there was something stirring, cared nothing what stirred or who suffered; the bilious antagonist to all men superior to himself, and who would pull down those above to his own level but never raise up to it those who lay below; the honest patriot willing to sink all minor differences in the one great aim, and ready to sacrifice himself for the good of his cause and class, but blind as a beetle as to the best methods: he saw them all, and he accepted all with that broad human love, that large and liberal allowance of differences, which made the charm of his character.

"They are good elements," he used to say, " badly mixed. Does not some one say that dirt is only matter in the wrong place? So these men as leaders would be pernicious enough, but a wise administration could utilise them. When Fourier could find an economic value in the *diablotin*, we need not fear for any one."

It was on this point that Joshua and the chief man of the London branch split. He was a purist, and gave his mind to tares. But Joshua thought more of the wheat, and believed in the larger power of good than of evil. He opposed all that narrow partisanship which goes only in one groove, and said, as the skilled workmen have lately said, that he would work with any one, no matter what his rank or politics, who would aid him and his order in securing the essentials for knowledge and decency of living. The more rabid and ultra of the politicians

attacked him, as he had been attacked in
the other society; but he held on in his own
broad, generous way. And though he never
got the ear of the International, because he
was so truly liberal, he had some little influence; and what influence he had ennobled
their councils as they have never been
ennobled since.

This is not speaking against the society.
I belong to it myself, and I am proud to do
so. But I have learnt from my friend to
distrust one-sided partisans, and to think all
questions best argued from their principles,
and the men who either support or oppose
them left out in the shade. Men don't
wilfully uphold the thing they know to be
bad. Take the stiffest Conservative of them
all—the man who believes in the divine
ordination of caste, and the absolute need

of preserving the fetichism of society as it is, even though, like Juggernaut, the great car of gentility crushes the whole working class beneath it — he may be, and is, sorry for the individuals ; but he maintains the existing order conscientiously. And to blackguard him, and call him blood-sucker, and all the names that hysterical men do call him, is simply childish anger, not manly argument. So, on the other side, the men who would make a revolution by fire and blood, as has been said, if necessary, though they too would be sorry for the individuals who had to suffer, yet they would feel the thing to be done so much more righteous than the suffering would be unrighteous, that they would sacrifice the few and the present to the good of the many and the future. And

these are no more " bloodthirsty scoundrels,"
and all the rest of it, than their opponents
After all, it is the same battle of strength which
goes on throughout creation—the struggle
for existence in class as in individuals ; and
" the good old rule, the royal plan " has its
meaning and its uses, in that it necessitates
endeavour ; which is the sole way by which
things human come to perfection.

CHAPTER VIII.

WE were sitting one evening at the night school which Joshua still kept up, the room full of men and women of what the world calls the worst kind, when the door was flung open with a clatter, and Joe Traill, shabbier and dirtier than ever, staggered in half-drunk. I do not know if I have said that Joshua had at last succeeded in getting him a situation, where he would have done well enough had he kept off drink; but he had not; and this was the upshot after about three months' fair sailing.

"It's no use, governor," he said to Joshua,

in his drunken way; "work and no lush too hard for me, governor! I'd got to fall soft!"

"Well Joe, my man, it seems that you have fallen soft enough this time; as soft as mud!" said Joshua. "However, sit down and make no noise. I will talk to you by-and-by."

"Not a copper!" said Joe, turning his pockets inside out and holding on by the tips. "I've come back like the devil, worse than I went!"

"All right, friend, but not just now; let me go on with what I have in hand, and then I'll attend to you."

But Joe was in that state when a man is either maudlin or quarrelsome. He was the latter; and partly because he had still sense enough to be ashamed of himself, and partly because he was pricking all over like a porcupine with the drink, and wanted to have it out with some one, he chose to try and fasten a quarrel on Joshua. So he set at him again; this time with some ribaldry I'll not lower myself to repeat. And again Joshua answered him mildly, but more authoritatively than before.

"Sit down," he said; and I don't think I ever heard his voice sound so hard and stern. "You've made a sore enough job of it for one day; don't add to your disgrace by folly."

Then the bad blood, the bad convict blood that never got quite clear away, boiled up in Joe, and he let out from his shoulder and struck Joshua on his head, at the side just above the ear. A dozen men rose at once; a dozen voices cursed and swore, some at

Joe for the blow, some yahing at Joshua for not returning it; women shrieked; the forms were upset as the men scrambled forward; and the quiet night-school was turned into a roaring Babel of tumult and violence. One brawny fellow—he too was a burglar, a man who might at any time develop into a murderer; but he had more fibre in him than poor, loose, slippery Joe, more to go upon as it were, and so could be held in hand better if once you could master his brutality—he squared up to the drunken creature, on whom already half-a-dozen hands were fiercely laid. But Joshua, who had turned white and sick-looking with the blow, laid his left hand on Jim's big arm, while he held out his right to Joe Traill, saying; "Why Joe! strike at a man, and your friend, for nothing! You must be

dreaming, my son, and a bad dream too!
Give us your hand, and wake up out of it!"

I can tell nothing more. There was
nothing perhaps in the words, but there was
that in the look of him, as he stood there
so white and yet so kingly, with one hand
keeping back Jim Graves, the other offered
to Joe squirming in the grasp of those who
held him, that acted like a spell on all the
room. There were men there, and women too,
who would have been ready to tear him in
pieces themselves if they had suspected for
an instant that his loving leniency was from
cowardice; but it was no coward who confronted the drunkard that had struck him,
who confronted that roaring, yelling crowd
of desperate men and women, and calmed
them all by his own unutterable dignity.
The same intense look that had come into

his face when, a little lad, he had questioned the parson in the church, when, a youth, he had prayed for a miracle in the Rocky Valley, came into his face now. He was as if raised into something more than man—so simple, so earnest as he was—so far above all common weaknesses, so near to God, so like to Christ!

Joe burst into tears, sobered and subdued; many of the women cried too, even that big coarse-mouthed Betsy Lyon, one of the most abandoned women of the district; while the men slunk together as it were, and most of them said a few rough words of praise, which, well meant as they were, sounded very far amiss at such a time. And then the police, attracted by the tumult, came up into the room; and, glad of an opportunity they had been looking for—after having been knocked about a good deal, for all that Joshua and I did our best to protect them—marched us both off to the station-house where we were locked up for the night, no bail being at hand.

The magistrate understood nothing of Joshua's defence next day, when he made it, but put him down with a severe rebuke. And as we had to be punished, reason or none, we were both sent to prison for a couple of weeks, as a caution to us to behave ourselves better in the future. To live according to Christ in modern Christendom was, as we found out, to be next thing to criminal, and at all events qualified for prison discipline. We don't understand anything about the Lazaruses and Simeons and Magdalenes of our own city. When we read of our Lord and Master going about among the bad people of His day, we say it was divine; when Joshua followed suit, he was locked up. Well, Christ was the criminal of His day; and Caiaphas the high priest, representing respectability and adhesion to the existing order of things, took Him in hand, and taught the multitude so well to feel how far He had erred against the morality of the day, that they asked for Barabbas rather than for him. And we have our Caiaphases in full vigour still.

We had not done with poor Joe. Mr. C.'s words came too true. The demon of drink had got possession of him, and he was no more his own master than if he had been a lunatic in Bedlam. During our fortnight's imprisonment he took everything he could lay his hands on—clothes, furniture, tools— every individual thing, he did!—and pawned them for drink : and when we were set at liberty, we found our place stripped.

I never had Joshua's patience, and I confess I was indignant. It did seem to me such wicked ingratitude, such lowness !

But when I flared up with sudden passion, and broke out against the thief for a rascal and a scoundrel, Joshua silenced me with a rebuke it was not in me to resist.

" Unto seventy times seven, John ?" he said, " I think we joined hands on that line ? " Then he added : " We must look that poor fellow up. He has got on to the incline, and, if not stopped, he will go down to perdition."

He took his hat and went out; and after many hours' search through all the worst haunts he knew of, brought Joe Traill back : and kept him.

I need not go over the whole after-history

of this wretched castaway. It is enough to say that again and again he fell into bad courses, and again and again Joshua forgave him. No trial was too severe for his Christian forbearance, his angelic patience. "Not to the sinless, but to the sinners," he used to say; and truly the sinners found it so!

This unwearied sweetness, this tenderness and hope that never failed, wrought their good work before too late; and the convicted thief, who but for Joshua would have ended his days at the hulks, if not at the gallows, died,—of the results of former poverty and vice, granted—so far at peace with the law as to die out of jail, and repeating softly, "God bless me and forgive me!"

These backslidings and failures were among the greatest difficulties of Joshua's work. Men and women, whom he had thought he had cleansed and set on a wholesome way of living, turned back again to the drink and the devilry of their lives. Excitement had become all in all to them; the monotony of virtue tired them, and they broke out into evil as a relief. But, fail as often and as badly as they might, they never chilled Joshua's heart, if they saddened him; as indeed they did. He forgave them everything; whether their sins had been against himself or against the law; and took them up where they had left him. Sometimes they laughed at him for his patience with them: sometimes they swore at him and refused his friendship; sometimes they cried and clung about him with pathetic but short-lived gratitude; and sometimes, but not often, they took his better lessons to heart and reformed altogether. For the most part, they just fluctuated—now bad, now good, as the fit took them and temptation was stronger than resolution. But, bad or good, he was ever the same to them—in the first case trying to win over, in the second helping to keep straight, and thankful if he succeeded ever so little in his endeavours.

The different reasons given by the various sectarians who came along, when any of his failures were afloat, were what I have said before. The Evangelicals said it was because he did not teach the Gospel; the Church people, because he was unconsecrated to the task; the Unitarians asked him, in calm disdain, how he could expect to do good, if he made no difference between vice and virtue but treated both alike? while the Charity Organization people talked of prosecuting him for his encouragement of mendicity, and spoke of him as the pest of the district and the cause of half the pauperism about, because he helped the poor in their need without enquiring into the merits of the case. And they all agreed that the weak spot in his system, and the cause of his failures, was just this—he was not a Christian.

In the midst of all Mary Prinsep came back on our hands. You may perhaps remember that her mistress had made a point of concealing her former life from every one ; in which she was justified, and for Mary's sake as much as for her own. Things had gone very well so far, and Mary had given satisfaction and worked hard to deserve it, when unfortunately that man who had known her only too well in the sorrowful days of her sin, came with his family to the house, on a visit of a day or two. All the

servants were marshalled into prayers morning and evening ; and naturally Mary with
them; face to face with the guests.   So there
it was—on the one side a dignified, handsome,
well-to-do gentleman, with respectable white
hair and a gold eye-glass, a wife and a
fine young family, a character to lose, and
a reputation for piety ; on the other, a poor
ignorant girl, abandoned by society, driven
by want into bad ways, but now doing her
best to get out of them.

It was an awkward meeting for him, and
he was afraid maybe of Mary's establish-
ing a claim, or telling what she knew.   There
he was, a guest in her master's house, with
his wife and eldest daughter, and under his
own name which she had never known, and
his private and official addresses both to be
got at.   It was an instinct of self-preserva-

tion, no doubt; but it was cowardly all the same; and, as usual, the weak one had to go to the wall. He made up an excellent story to explain how it was that he knew the girl's former life. It was a story to his credit as a Christian gentleman somehow, and he told it out of sheer regard for his good friends who had been so shamefully imposed on. And even when the lady confessed, as she did, that she had known the main fact of Mary's history, she was urged so strongly to get rid of her that she consented, partly in a vague kind of belief that she had been imposed on and that Mary was worse than she appeared and capable of all manner of unknown crimes, partly by the force of respectability and the need of keeping up blameless appearances. So, as the right thing to do considering her position and

what she owed her family and her own character, this lady—good Christian as she was,
going to church regularly twice on Sunday,
and taking the sacrament once a month—
turned the poor creature out of doors again ;
and she, keeping the gentleman's secret loyally,
came back to us, as the only friends she had.

She was something different to us from
any other girl that Joshua had been
the means of rescuing, and we both felt
that she had a stronger claim somehow, on
our exertions and affections. Other women
came and went, and Joshua helped them and
got them work, and did what he could for
them, and always kept up a kindly interest
in them, and the like of that; but they
were not to us what Mary was ; for she was
like our own sister. So, when she came
back, it was just a family sorrow somehow ;

but, to me at least, it was a bit of a joy too. But you see since we had got into that trouble about Joe, and had been locked up, we had been worse off than ever. Masters would not employ us; mates would not work with us—we were "jail birds" to them ; and the Union turned us out. Joshua held on though, and we got day-jobs; but we were often hungry and often weary; yet Joshua never let me sink into despair, nor was he ever near it himself, and we managed to scrape along somehow. Still, our present poverty made poor Mary's return embarrassing, though she didn't see it all.

"It is of no use, Joshua," she said, sitting on a chair and leaning her head on her hand disconsolately: "once lost, you are done for in this world! There is nothing for me but the old way; it is all I have left!"

I remember so well when she said this. The sun had come round to our window; for it was a summer's evening; and it came into the room and fell on her, as she sat with her bonnet off, and her fair hair partly fallen about her face. She had very fine hair, and she knew it. I remember too that her dress was some kind of blue, and that she looked like a picture there is in the National Gallery; and I thought, if only some one who could save her really, and lift her up for ever out of the past, could but see her now!

"Courage, Mary, and patience," said Joshua.

"Yes, I know all that; but the ways and means?" said Mary, raising her eyes to him. "What can I do, Joshua? To get my bread any way but the old way I must creep into a house under false pretences, and then be always afraid of being found out; and if I am found out I am sure to be turned off. No one will have me who knows about me, if I work ever so hard, or try to do my duty ever so faithfully."

"One failure is not final," said Joshua. "While we have a home, you have one too; you are our sister, remember. Only have faith, and as I said before courage and patience; and beware of the first step back!"

"Ah, Joshua!" said Mary, "you are an angel!"

"No," he answered smiling, "I am only a man trying to live by principle."

But if he was not an angel he was not far off being one.

It was difficult to know what to do for the best for Mary. We kept her for as long as we could, she doing our chores for us in the old way for her meat and room; and then Joshua raised funds—I can scarce understand how, but the poorest of the people helped, as well as the best off —and somehow, enough was got together to establish her in a small sweet-stuff shop in East-street close to Church-court. To help her with the rent we went to lodge with her; which suited both her and ourselves; for you see we had got accustomed to her, and she to us, and she knew our ways, and was always good and helpful. People talked, of course; but then people talk about anything, reason or none, that is out of the common by ever so small a line; and no man who has taken an independent path can escape the comment of the crowd accustomed to only one way. The old report that we were living with a woman of bad character crept about again, and got down to our dear Cornish homes. You may be sure it made our mothers bad enough when they heard it; but I don't think they quite believed it, though they thought it right to send us a warning, as if they did; and if they did, then they believed what was not true. As for ourselves, we had our own consciences and Mary's salvation to keep us up; and with these it mattered little what any one else chose to say. As Joshua said, we had not set out in our endeavour to realise Christ for the sake of gain, but for the sake of the right; and if we had to suffer, we must; but the right was not to be abandoned because of it.

CHAPTER IX.

LORD X., (I may not in common honour give his name; a man however—so far I may say—notorious for his philanthropy of an unsteady and spasmodic kind, and for a certain restless curiosity to see into the inside of different social circles)—this lord, in his wanderings among the East-end poor, had come across Joshua in his little kingdom of endeavour in Church-court. And as no one could come in contact with him, without feeling that inexplicable charm which is inseparable from great earnestness and self-devotion, it is to be supposed that Lord X.

among the rest was attracted to the man as he was. Or maybe it was only a poor kind of curiosity, not sympathy; as I have since believed. However that may be, he and Joshua met; and a friendship was struck up between them on the spot. I use the word advisedly; for though the one was a peer of the realm, and the other only an artisan—not learned in the scholarly way of a gentleman; not refined in the same way perhaps as a gentleman, so far as manner and little observances went; a man speaking with a provincial accent, and dressed in fustian and coarse clothes—yet he was fit to take his place with the finest gentleman in the land; and even the finest lady would have found but little in him to ridicule and much to respect. And I will do both Lord and Lady X. the credit of sincerity in

the beginning, when, as I said, the friendship between him and them was struck up.

Then it must be remembered, that Joshua
was one of the handsomest men you could
see in a long summer's day ; a real man ; no
sickly, effeminate, half-woman, but a tall,
broad-shouldered, deep-chested fellow, largely
framed, and with that calm self-control, that
steady unfeverish energy, which seemed as
if it could carry the world before it. And
maybe his good looks influenced his new
acquaintances in the beginning, even more
than they themselves knew. However that
might be, they made up to him, and seemed
as though they would have been his best
friends all through.

"You want a background, Mr. Davidson,"
said Lord X., one day when he called on
him at our lodgings. "All human nature

resolves itself into a mathematical formula; x plus y represents a quantity unattainable by x alone."

"But what background can I get, my lord?" returned Joshua. "It sounds a strange confession to make, but no one will work with me. Sects keep only to themselves or their affiliations; and I, who belong to no sect, am looked on as an enemy by all because I am an enemy to none."

"Putting sectarianism aside for the moment, you can do nothing without the sanction of society," said Lord X. "No movement can succeed which is not backed by men of birth and money."

Joshua smiled. "This remark does not apply to the roots, my lord, I suppose?" he said; "only to the growth and development?"

"Oh!" said Lord X., carelessly, "a low fellow might strike out an idea, but it would want a man of position to develop it."

"Well, perhaps you are right," Joshua answered. "For, after all, Christianity owes more to Paul than to Jesus; and the Pauline development has struck deeper and spread wider than the Christ original."

"Just so," said Lord X.

"The one being example, both difficult to follow and subversive of the existing state of things; the other dogma which ranks the intellectual acceptance of a creed above the revolutionary ethics on which it is based," said Joshua.

"But, Mr. Davidson!" remonstrated Lord X., "surely even you, enthusiast as you are, must acknowledge that it would be impossible to go back to the practices of early Christian times? The staff and the scrip were all very well in their day, but they would scarcely do now. Society has become more complex and intricate since then; it would be out of all question to have the common purse and live in the barbaric simplicity of apostolic times. Times change, and manners with them."

"Which is just my difficulty, my lord," said Joshua. "For if modern society is right, then Christ was wrong; and we have to look elsewhere than to Him for a solution of our moral and social problems."

"I would not pronounce so crudely as that," said Lord X. "Say rather that a further development may reconcile our differences."

"So be it, sir; yet if this is so, we are still in the same position as before, and the life of Christ, as related in the Bible, is not the absolute example for us to follow."

"About that you must form your own opinion," said Lord X., with a certain cynical indifference not pleasant to witness. "What you may or may not believe of the Bible is a question for yourself alone to decide : it can have no interest for any one else. What has an interest, however, is your mode of dealing with the great social problems in which you have bestirred yourself; and, going back to our starting-point, I say again that you can do nothing if society does not assist you."

Joshua smiled a little sadly. "And I have only the same answer to make, my lord," he said. "No one will help me; and my work, such as it is, stands alone."

"Then I think, Mr. Davidson, that it

must be your own fault," said Lord X. "There are liberal denominations to which your spirit of inquiry would not be alien; why cannot you coalesce with them? The Broad Church do not nail their colours to your old enemy, dogma; and the Unitarians are not superstitious."

"But the Unitarians above all demand respectability of life," said Joshua. "Having abandoned that wide harbour, the Atonement, they are obliged to anchor themselves on morality. My poor lost sheep would come off but badly before the rigid tribunal of Unitarian morality; and the Broad Church, though more humane perhaps, requires at the least repentance. But the men and women I have to do with are without a sense of sin—people who fail again and again, and whom nothing but the utmost

"Then I do not see much use in your attempts," said Lord X. "I myself would do all I could to rescue the poor wretches one sees in the courts and alleys from the filth and misery in which they live. But when I find I am doing no real good, and that they go wrong again, I leave them to their fate and mark them off as hopeless. You must draw a line, Mr. Davidson! For the sake of society, you must show some difference in your estimate of men. To treat the deserving and the undeserving alike is gross injustice. Some of these wretches are more like brutes than men. I would clear them all out like rats; and with no more compunction than if they were rats."

"I do not agree with you, my lord. I

believe that more harm has been done by condemnation than ever would come through tolerance. By love alone can the world be saved."

" Love ? Rubbish ! " said Lord X. " The laws must be obeyed, and society supported."

" Only in so far as it is just," put in Joshua.

" If by just you mean equality, pardon me if I say that you talk nonsense," said Lord X. " You might as well say that nature is unjust, because a grove of oaks needs more space than a row of turnips, as that man is to blame because he has lifted himself into classes of which the superiors have more than the inferiors. If it had not been for this injustice, as you call it, we should never have had a superior class at all, and the world would have gone on for ever in one dead level of mediocrity, where no one shone, and no one was obscured."

"Granted," said Joshua. "But you having developed into stars and suns, what we want is, that you should help the poor dark spheres on the same way."

Lord X. laughed. "I doubt the power and I question the wisdom of that," he said. "Help them to be cleanly and virtuous and content with their natural position, if you like; but I for one do not go further."

"And Christ and history do, my lord," said Joshua.

"Mr. Davidson, you are incorrigible!" said Lord X., jocularly; "but happily your opinions do not vitiate your good works, and I will help you in these where I can."

"Thank you, my lord," said Joshua simply : "I shall hold you to your promise. And yet you must understand that I hope far more from the union and organization of the working classes together, than from any extraneous aid whatever; only we take all kinds."

"In which you are wise," said Lord X., drily. "You would get on but poorly among yourselves I fancy, if it were not for Us."

Joshua did not answer. He said afterwards that, having made his declaration honestly, he felt it would have been ungenerous to have carried the conversation further on that line. While accepting my lord's help it was scarcely the thing to depreciate it; so the talk then drifted or rather settled on all that he had been doing in Church-court and the neighbourhood—on his night-school, his charities, his hospitality to thieves and the like ; and the results ; those whom he might fairly count as his successes, with those who had been as yet his failures. He never allowed more than this "as yet." "While there is a gate open to them, there is always the hope that they will enter in by it," he used to say. "What men are taught of Christ in heaven—that no shame, no disgrace, no sin can make Him turn away His face from those who seek Him—so ought they to find here on earth in human pity and human love. If we were more patient, we should have more power over each other, and there would be fewer failures."

"You mean, if we were gods we should act in a godlike manner," said Lord X., with that curious mixture of cynicism and philanthropy, kindness and satire, earnestness and levity, that characterised him.

"No," Joshua answered; "I mean only that, if we did our best possible as men, we should make a better job of life altogether both for ourselves individually and for the world at large."

"You must come and see me, Mr. Davidson," said Lord X., suddenly rising and drawing on his gloves. "Lady X. will be charmed to see you, I am sure. She is immensely interested in all sorts of social questions, and I shall be delighted to present you. You will be a new reading to her," he added, and smiled.

"I will come and be read," said Joshua; "and I hope to a good end. If I can interest you, and your friends through you, my lord, I shall have done something."

This was the first time that I had seen Joshua really elated with hope of help from the outside. He knew that Lord X. was a man of immense wealth, and that he could, if he would, do wonders for his poor friends. But he did not know how shallow his philanthropic zeal was; how much more a matter of mere amusement than of vital principle. His work among the poor was the work of a superior; and his estimate of his own class, and therefore of himself as a peer, was so curiously great, that he thought his very presence among them ought to prove a kind of balm and moral styptic to all their wounds. He was willing to give when the fit took him; but he would have resented the doctrine of duty, or the right to take. The poor were as curious specimens to him. He never regarded them as men and women like himself and his class. He scarcely gave them credit for ordinary human feeling even; for he used to say that affections and nerves were both matters of education and refinement, and that the uneducated and unrefined neither loved nor felt as the others. Perhaps he was right. I am not physiologist enough to know much about nerves and pain and the difference of education, so far as that goes; but I think I have seen as much real affection, as much passionate self-abandoning, self-sacrificing love among the poor as there is among the rich. It may be more uncouth, its demonstration more simple too, and less elegantly expressed, but it is there all the same, and maybe in fuller quantity than with fashionable folks who really seem too idle and dispersed to be able to love with either vigour or concentration.

Furthermore, philanthropy to Lord X. was an occupation and a reputation. He had no turn for abstract politics, no head for diplomacy, no taste for literature; he was not an artist nor a mechanician, but he was ambitious, and he liked distinction. So, dabbling among the poor, and touching the grave social problems besetting them delicately, following them to their haunts and relieving their immediate distress, pleased both his kind heart and his vanity; and he did substantial good of a fragmentary kind, if his motives would scarce bear severe scrutiny.

For myself I did not augur much from the association. Less spiritual and less single-minded than my friend, I could also judge better than he of his own power of fascination. Hence I could discern more clearly than he, how much of Lord X.'s offer of help was the genuine movement of his own soul, and how much was due to the curiosity and amusement which the study of a life and character at once so fresh and whole-hearted as his awakened and promised. But it was not for me to speak, or throw cold water on what might turn out to be such a boon to the cause. If Joshua had wanted my advice, he would have asked it. As he did not ask it, I considered him best able to judge for himself. And yet sometimes I have been sorry that I did not speak.

CHAPTER X.

THIS was Joshua's first introduction into a wealthy house of the upper classes; and from the retinue of servants in their gorgeous liveries thronging the hall, to the little lap-dog on its velvet cushion, the luxury and lavishness he saw everywhere almost stupified him. To a man earning, say some twenty-five shillings a week, and living on less than half—sharing with those poorer than himself, and content to go short that others might be satisfied — the revelation of Lord X.'s house was a sharp and positive pain. The starvation he, the nobleman, had seen in his wanderings — starvation in all probability relieved for to-day; but to-morrow and the day after and for all future time, till the pauper's grave closed over all?—and then had come back to an abundance, a fastidiousness, of which the very refuse would have been salvation to hundreds; the miserable dwellings he visited, mere styes of filth, immodesty, and vice, where the seeds of physical disease and moral corruption are sown broadcast and from earliest infancy— and then returned to a dwelling like a fairy palace, where every nook and corner was perfect, redolent of all kinds of sweetness and loveliness—to a man of the people like Joshua, fairly oppressive in its richness and grandeur; the gaunt and famine-wasted men and women and children that he had so often met, the little ones brutally treated, half starved, sworn at, and knocked about, swarming through reeking courts and alleys where the very air of heaven was poisonous— and the lady's lap-dog, with its dainty food, its tender care, well washed, combed, curled, scented, adorned, on a velvet footstool, a toy bought for it to play with : and that man and that woman—this lord and lady—were professing Christians, went regularly to church, believed that Christ was very God, and that every word of the Bible was inspired ! It was habit; but at first sight it looked incomprehensible to one who lived among the poor, and was of them.

Lady X. soon came into the room where Joshua and Lord X. were. She was a tall, fair, languid woman, kindly natured but selfish, dissatisfied with her life as it was yet unable to devise anything better for herself, having no interest anywhere, without children, and evidently not as much in love with her husband as model wives usually are : a woman whose intelligence and physique clashed, the one being restless and the other indolent. Every now and then she took up her husband's " cases," partly out of complaisance to him, partly from profound weariness with her life, and also from the natural kind-heartedness which made her like to do good-natured things and to give pleasure to others. But she soon abandoned them and set them adrift. She was a woman with great curiosity but no tenacity ; full of a soft sensual kind of passion that led her into danger as much from idleness as from vice ; she loved out of idleness, and worked out of idleness. It was a gain to her to be interested in anything—whether it was the fashion of the day or the salvation of a human soul; but there was no spirit of self-sacrifice in her, and she would have considered it an impertinence if she had been asked to do a hair's-breadth more than she desired of her own free-will. Had she been born poor, she might have been a grand woman; as she was, she was just a fine lady whose nobler nature was stifled under the weight of idleness and luxury.

But she liked Joshua, and took to him kindly.

She gave him at that first interview a really handsome sum of money for his poorer friends; she promised clothes and soup-tickets, books for his school, toys for his children, good food for his sick. The simple yet so grand earnestness of the man interested her, and she too felt as every one else did, that here was a master-spirit which had a claim to all men's reverence and admiration. She was not satisfied with this first visit, but Joshua must go to see her again ; and after he had been there twice, she of herself offered to come and see him in his lodgings, over the little sweet-stuff shop which Mary Prinsep kept. And Joshua did not forbid her.

Was there ever such an incongruity ? The street—East-street—in which we lived, was too narrow for her carriage to come down, so she had to walk the distance to Joshua's rooms. And I shall never forget the sight. Her dainty feet were clothed in satin on which glittered buckles that looked like diamonds ; her dress was of apple-blossom-coloured silk that trailed behind her ; her bonnet seemed to be just a feather and a veil; she wore some light lace thing about her that looked like a cloud more than a fabric; and her arms and neck were covered with chains and lockets and bracelets. She was like a fairy queen among the gnomes and blackamoors of an underground mine, like a sweet-scented rose-bush in the midst of a refuse heap as she came picking her way with courage, but with exaggerated delicacy, her footman in his blue and silver at her back, and the mob of the street staring, too much astonished at such an apparition to jeer.

When she came into the **little** shop and asked for Joshua, I was standing in the doorway (it was on a Sunday) between the shop and Mary's back room; and for the first time I saw Mary in an ugly light. She turned quite white as the lady came in, and instead of answering, looked round to me with an agony in her face that was inde- scribable.

"Yes, madam," I said coming forward; "he is up-stairs."

"Do you want him, ma'am?" then asked Mary, the look of pain still in her large fixed eyes; and I thought that the lady, looking at her—for Mary was young and very pretty, as I have said—looked uneasy too. At all events, she looked haughty.

"Yes," she said; but she turned and spoke to me, not to Mary. "Have the good- ness to tell him that Lady X. wants to speak to him."

I ran upstairs and told him; and Joshua, without changing his countenance one whit, as if lords and ladies in gorgeous array were our natural visitors and what we were used

to every day, came down and greeted the
lady as he would have greeted the baker's
wife—neither more nor less respectfully;
which means, that he was respectful to
every one.

Lady X. made a step forward when he
came into the shop, and the blood flew
over her face as she gave him her hand.

"Now, you must let me see where you
live, and how you do such wonders," she
said, with the most undefinable but unmis-
takable accent of coaxing in the voice.

And Joshua saying quietly; "Are you not
too fine to come up our stairs, Lady X.?
—we do our best to keep them clean,
Mary, don't we? but they are not used to
such-like feet on them;" gave her his hand
smiling.

"They will be used to mine. I hope, often,"

said my lady kindly. "You know I have taken a great interest in your work, Mr. Davidson, and I am going to help where I can."

"If you will come this way then, my lady, I will show you all I have on hand at the present moment," said Joshua moving towards the stairs.

And again the lady blushed ; and her long silk skirts trailed behind her with a curious rustling noise ; and we heard her light boot-heels go tap, tap, up the stairs, and her chains and trinkets jingle.

Then Mary turned to me, and said with a wild kind of look ; "John ! John ! she is here for no good ! She will harm more than she helps. What call has she to come here ? who wants her ? She will only do us all a mischief !"

She turned her face to the window and burst into tears.

"Mary! what ails you?" I said, vaguely; for I was shocked, and did not rightly understand her. I seemed to feel something I could not give a name to—a pain and a queer kind of doubt; but indeed it was all chaotic, and all I knew was that I was sorry. "You know," I went on trying to comfort her, "that money and worldly influence at Joshua's back would give him all he wants. His hands are so weak now for want of both these things. Why should we be sorry, dear, that he has the chance of them?"

"She has come for no good!" was all that Mary would say; and I could only wonder at an outburst unlike anything I had ever seen before.

My lady stayed a long time upstairs, and poor Mary's agony during her visit never relaxed. At last she came down, flushed and radiant. Her eyes were softer and darker, her face looked younger and more tender; she even glanced kindly at me as she passed me, saying to Joshua in a voice as sweet as a silver bell; "And this is the John you have been telling me about?—he looks a good fellow!—and is this Mary?" but she was not quite so tender to Mary; and she added, in rather a displeased tone of voice; "Girl! you look very young to keep house by yourself, and have young men lodgers!"

"Ah, my lady, you forget that our girls have not the care taken of them that yours have," said Joshua gently. "So soon as a girl of ours can get her living, she does."

"Well, I hope that Mary will be a good girl, and do you credit," said my lady coldly.

She shook hands then with Joshua, but, with her hand still in his, turned to him and, with the sweetest smile I have ever seen on woman's face, said in the same strange caressing way; "I must ask you to be kind enough to take me to my carriage, Mr. Davidson. I think my footman must have gone to keep the coachman company; and I should scarcely like to go down the street alone."

"Certainly not," said Joshua, and led her, still holding her hand, out from the shop and into the little street to where her carriage was waiting for her.

"Mind the shop for me, John," said Mary; and with a great sob she ran away and shut herself up in her own room.

She would have been ashamed I know, to let Joshua see that she was crying, and all for nothing, too; only because a fine lady, smelling of sweet scents and wearing a rich silk gown, had passed through the shop.

As for him, he came back without a ruffle on his quiet, mild face. There was no flush of gratified vanity on it; nothing but just that inward, absorbed look, that look of peace and love which beautified him at all times. As he passed through, he looked round for Mary; but I told him she was bad with her head; and as this had the effect of sending him into her room to look after her, poor Mary's attempt at conceal-ment came to nothing. But I don't think Joshua found out why she was crying.

Many a day after this my lady's carriage came to the entrance of our wretched street, and my lady herself, like a radiant vision, picked her way among garbage and ruffianism down to the little sweet-stuff shop where ha'pennyworths of "bulls'-eyes" were sold to young children by a girl who had once been a street-walker, and where the upstairs rooms were tenanted by two journeymen carpenters. It was an anomaly that could not last; but the very sharpness of the contrast gave it interest in her eyes; and while the novelty continued it was like a scene out of a play in which she was the heroine. So, at least, I judged her; and the more I think of the whole affair, the more sure I feel that I am right.

And then Joshua's handsome face and

dignity of look and manner might count for
something.

She (the lady) was truly good and helpful
to Joshua all the time this fad of hers
lasted; for that it was only a fad, without
stability or roots, the sequel proved. She
brought him clothes and money, and seemed
ready to do all she could for him. He had
only to tell her that he wanted such and
such help, and she gave it, aye, like a
princess !

What took place between them neither
I nor any one can say. Joshua never opened
his lips on the subject ; and after that day, by
tacit consent all round, the name of Lord and
Lady X. was a dead letter among us. All
I know is, that one day, when she had come
down to our place as so often now, my lady,
flushed, haughty, trembling too, but changed

somehow, with a sad, disordered face instead of the half-sleepy sweetness usual to it, came downstairs—not this time holding Joshua's hand; he following her, pale and troubled-looking; that she passed through the little shop quickly and impatiently, with never a glance towards Mary or me; that at the door she turned round, and said sharply; "You need not give yourself the trouble, Mr. Davidson, to come with me—I can find my way alone;" and that Joshua answered with more tenderness and humility of tone and manner than I had ever seen or heard in him before; "My lady, I must disobey you: I cannot let you go through the street alone." And that he followed her out, bare-headed, but at a little distance from her—not beside her.

This was the last time we saw her; nor

did Lord X. keep up any association with my friend. And I heard afterwards, quite accidentally, that he had said soon after this, he really "could not countenance that man Davidson : he was too offensively radical in his opinions, and a presuming fellow besides."

But word came to us both that my lady had found out all about Mary, and that she had expressed herself insulted and revolted at Joshua's allowing her to enter a house kept by such a creature.

"It was all very well to be compassionate and helpful," she had said ; "but no amount of charity justified that man Davidson in his proceedings with such a woman. Or, if he chose to associate with her himself, he ought to have warned her (her ladyship), that *she* should not have made the mistake of speaking to her as to a proper person."

So this first and last attempt at aristocratic co-operation fell to the ground; and Society peremptorily refused to endorse a man who had set himself to live the life after Christ.

If Joshua was sorry for the loss he had so mysteriously sustained, poor Mary was not. All during the lady's visits she had drooped and pined, till I thought she was in a bad way, and going to be worse. Ah! this was a bitter time to me, for I loved her like my own; and I loved Joshua and his work and his life better than my own life; and I was perplexed, and in a manner torn to pieces, among so many feelings. But she revived after the day when the lady passed through the shop with her sad, proud, disordered face, and when Joshua came back from seeing her to her carriage, like a man who has had a blow and is still dazed by it. She waited on him after this, more assiduously than ever. She seemed to live only to please him. The place was the very perfection of cleanliness. Even my lady's palace could not have been more wholesome or more pure. The squalor of the shell, so to speak, and the poverty of the inside, was concealed or made to be forgotten by the exquisite neatness and cleanliness with which it was all kept; and when Joshua's countenance came back again, as it did after awhile, to its usual sweet serenity, Mary's also came to its peace, and the cloud that had hung over it like a distemper passed away.

"It will not do, John!" he said to me one

day, some time after: "for the aristocracy to come down to the poor is a mistake. They are different creatures altogether, with different laws of honour and morality among themselves from what we know anything about. And the gulf is too wide to be bridged over by just one here, and another there, coming like the old Israelitish spies among us, to see the nakedness of the land. They do a little good for the time, but it is good that bears no blessing with it, and is not lasting. We must work up by ourselves into a state nearer to them in material good; but not," he added, as if by an after-thought, "in looseness of principle. That, however, has come only from idleness; and if great people had imperative duties and the abso- lute need of exertion, we should hear of fewer divorce scandals, fewer turf catas-

trophes, and the like, than we do now.
However, that is not our affair. We are
here to work on our own account, not to
judge of others."

"It is an old saying, Joshua, but a true
one, 'extremes meet,'" said I. "The very
poor have no taste for refined pleasure, and
indeed no power of indulging it if they
had; and the very rich, sated with all that is
given to them by their position, devise new
excitements of an ignoble kind. I suppose
that is something like it?"

"I suppose so," he answered. "At all
events, there can be no such thing as level-
ling down. It would be no righteousness to
bring the rich, the refined, the well educated
down to the level of the poor; but to raise
up the masses, and to impose on the upper
classes positive duties, this is the only way

in which the difference between high and low can be lessened. And if this can be done free of national revolt and bloodshed, it will be a godlike work, and the blessed solution of the greatest difficulty the world has seen yet. It cannot be a good thing that some men have to work till all the strength of intellect is worked out of them, while others are lapped in such idleness that all theirs is either bemused and stagnated, or turned to evil issues for want of being wholesomely used. Come how it may, it has to come—this more equal distribution of the better things of life. I do not mean that the duchess will have to share her velvet cushions with the seamstress; but it has to be that, either by education or improved machinery, or both, there will not be the enormous difference there is now between the duchess and the seamstress. We have made a great parade lately of our sympathy with the North, on the ground of emancipation; but Society here in London holds slaves as arbitrarily and as cruelly as ever the Southern planters did; and its vested interests, however demoralising, are as sacred to us as were the vested interests of the planter to him. I will never again try a fraternal union with a rich house. When the working-men have their political and social rights, and have utilised their leisure to refine and elevate, to beautify and adorn their lives, then, when we are radically equal, we can meet as men and brothers. As we are now, we are experiments to some, mere temporary amusements to others, inferiors to all; and we pin our faith to a straw— hang our golden hopes on gossamer —

when we look for vital co-operation from them."

"I thought Joshua would find her out in time," was Mary's comment. "I took stock of her from the first, and saw she was no good."

CHAPTER XI.

I HAVE said so much of the personal charities of Joshua that I seem to have thrown into the shade, by comparison, his political life and action; and yet this was the more important of the two. The extreme section of republican working men, though they did not go in for his religious views, made use of his political zeal; and when work was bad to get, sometimes he was sent as a delegate, sometimes he went of his own accord, to the various towns that needed either encouragement or awakening; where he gave lectures on the necessity of labour keeping a close front against the serried ranks of capital; on the lawfulness and desirability of trades' unions and strikes, when occasion demands; on the political worth of a republic that grows naturally out of monarchy and oligarchy, as manhood grows out of childhood; on the need of the working classes raising themselves to a higher level in mind and circumstance than that which they occupy now; on the beauty of social and moral freedom; and on the right of each man to a fair share of the primary essentials for good living. And all this was mixed up with that fervid practical Christianity of his, which gave a new and holier aspect to every question he handled.

Joshua believed in the religion of politics. He often said that, were Christ to come again in this day, He would be more of a politician than a theologian; and that He would teach men to work for the coming of the kingdom of heaven on earth, rather through the general elevation of the material condition of the masses than by either ritual or dogma.

"You can't make a man a saint in mind," I have heard him say more than once, "when you keep him like a beast in body;" and "higher wages, better food, better lodgment, and better education will do more to make men real Christians than all the churches ever built."

No man was more convinced than he that sin and misery are the removable results of social circumstances, and that poverty, ignorance, and class-distinctions consequent, are at the root of all the crimes and wretched-

ness afloat. The evil lying in that great
curse of partial civilisation—that upas tree
of caste—by which this Christian world of
ours, with its religion of brotherhood and
socialism, is overshadowed, pained him most
of all. The caste of the rich, with its product, the class antagonism of the poor—
what a sorry satire on the religion of
Jesus of Nazareth, that poor, unlearned
man of the people, whom we have exalted into God and now worship with
gorgeous ceremonial, while despising every
one of the social doctrines He and His
disciples preached! However, Joshua did
his best to rouse men to a consciousness of
Christ, and to the acceptance of His teaching
of human equality; and though steadily opposed to all doctrines of violence, was always
the passionate upholder of the doctrine of

duty on the one side and the theory of rights on the other.

He had often a sore time of it. His discourses roused immense antagonism, and he was sometimes set upon and severely handled by the men to whom he spoke. I have seen him left for dead twice in the rough monarchical towns. But he worked as the Master had worked before him; simply changing the methods to be more in harmony with the times; going on his way calm, unshaken, cheerful, ever ready to face the worst and take what danger might arise without blenching; of a steadfast heart and a loyal spirit; looking up to God, living after Christ, and loving the humanity that blackguarded and nearly killed him as his reward. Tears are in my eyes, rough man as I am, when I remember Joshua Davidson, his life and works, and what the world he lived but to better said of him and did to him. I have known swindlers and murderers more gently entreated. Of a truth, the age of martyrs has not passed away; as any one may prove in his own person who will set himself to enlarge the close boroughs of thought, and to rectify the injustice of society.

The war broke out between France and Prussia, and at the first the tide of liberal sympathies went with Prussia, as representing opposition to the Empire. But as time went on, sides changed, and moderates backed up Prussia, while the ultra-Tories and the Republicans went with France; the one hoping to see the Empire restored, the other longing for the establishment of liberty. And Joshua's sympathies changed with the rest I ought perhaps to have made more than I have done of his intimacy with certain foreign socialists and reformers. Félix Pyat I have already spoken of. He was one of our warmest friends ; and, to go to a very materialistic part of the subject, his association with us both was of great value, not only for the sake of the man himself, but also for the opportunity he afforded us of learning the French language.

When the Commune declared itself on the eighteenth of March, none but those in the centre of advanced political feeling can tell what passionate hopes were awakened in the men who care for liberty and believe in social progress. Comtists, Internationalists, Secularists, Socialists, Republicans, by what name soever the doctrine of liberty and brotherhood may be proclaimed, we all looked over

to Paris with an anxiety that was as painful
as if we stood watching the struggles of a
beloved friend with our own hands bound.
There were men whom that time sent mad
with hope and fear; and some that I could
name are now lying cold in their graves
for sorrow at the failure of the righteous
cause. The Commune, successful in Paris,
meant the emancipation of the working
clases here, and later on the peaceable establishment of the Republic; which we all
believe *has to come*, whether peaceably
established or not.

On the nineteenth of March, Joshua
resolved to go over to Paris, to help, so far
as he could, in the cause of humanity. I
never saw him so full of enthusiasm. Every
now and then, especially of late, his hope, if
not his zeal, had slackened a little before

the magnitude of the task he had undertaken at home. Alone as he was, not only unsupported by any influential men whatsoever, but actively opposed by many, he found his work of amelioration very hard, and the results unsatisfactory. But to help in the establishment of an organised liberty like the Commune—that seemed the best thing any man loving his fellow-men could do; and accordingly, he and I agreed to go over at once. And poor Mary Prinsep was broken hearted. But, sorry as he was to give her sorrow, his duty was too clear before him to let him hesitate; and, stifling whatever grief of private affection he might leave behind him, he set his face toward Paris; and after some difficulties and dangers we arrived there, "let into the trap" as so many before and after us.

As this is not a history of the Commune it is not necessary to say much about the leaders. Some he loved like his very brothers; others, chiefly of the noisier sort, he distrusted as leaders, and would rather have seen subordinate to better-balanced minds. He might not too, have always agreed even with the men he loved. Being men, they were fallible; but they did honestly for the best, and the abuse hurled at them—a "nest of miscreants," a "handful of brigands," and the like—was as untrue as it was illogical. There were among the Communist leaders men as noble as ever lived upon earth; men, whatever their special creed, the most after the pattern of Christ in their faithful endeavour to help the poor and to raise the lowly, to rectify the injustice of conventional distinctions, and to give all men an equal chance of being happy, virtuous, and human.

Never had Paris been so free from crime as during the administration of the Commune —never so pure. All the vice which had disgraced the city ever since the congenial Empire had existed, was swept clean out of it; and not the most reckless vilifiers of these latter-day Christ-men could make out a case of peculation, of greed, or of uncleanness among them. Skilled artisans abandoned their lucrative callings for the starvation-pay of a franc and a half a day, and set themselves —not to amass wealth, not to gain power, nor to live in luxury and pleasure—but to plan for the best for their fellow-men, and to sketch out a future glorious alike for France and the whole world. The working man vindicated then his claim to be entrusted with his own self-government; and one of the brightest pages of modern history, in spite of all its mistakes, is that wherein the artisan government of '71 wrote its brief but noble record on the heart of Paris.

The most fatal thing of that time, however, was the unconquerable distrust of the people. Long used to tyranny and treachery as they had been, they seemed unable to accept any man as a true patriot, not plotting underhand for his own advantage. They trusted no one — not even their sworn and tested friends. And we can scarcely wonder at it. Twenty years of Louis Napoleon, the military command of Trochu, the history of the past Imperial administration and the present Imperial war, had eaten into their very hearts, and taken all the faith out of them. And the consequence was, that even the men now heading the great liberation movement, the best and most unselfish of the " sinless Cains " of history, were suspected by the very city they were sacrificing themselves to save.

But Paris was mad—mad with despair, with famine, with shame, disease, excitement. The gaunt frames, the hollow cheeks, the wild eyes that met you at every turn, were eloquent witnesses of the state of men's minds; and I shall never forget the mournful impression it all made on me. No one looked sane, save the leaders, and perhaps a few of us more cool-headed Anglo-Saxons. The Poles, who had flocked in to take part in a cause they identified with their own broken nationality, added the fever of their political despair to the fire consuming the vitals of the Parisians; the Italians poured

in their bitter hatred to the priests as oil
on flames—emblems to them of tyranny,
treachery, ignorance, and persecution they
could not be brought to acknowledge even
the good that is in them, but were ever their
unrelenting enemies; the republicans of all
nations gathered into the struggling city,
each with his own specific and his own de-
sires; everywhere was fierce excitement, and
the conflict of hope and fear, high endeavour and deep despair; while it grew
clearer and clearer, as the days passed by,
that the cause of the freedom of Paris, and
with Paris of Europe—the cause of the
rights and better organisation of labour—was
lost for the hour, and that hope only was left
for the future. The city was overmatched,
and liberty was doomed. It was but a question of time; the Commune had to die, and

it resolved to die fighting and unsurrendered.

Of all the Communists, Delescluze was the one Joshua loved most, because he esteemed him most; and this, not forgetting his old loyalty and friendship to Félix Pyat, nor denying reverence and love to many others. But there was something special in Delescluze. His heroic spirit, his martyr's life, his unbroken courage, his unquenchable faith, and that quiet sadness which seemed like the sadness of a prophet—all that he was, and had been, raised one's admiration more than any other man among them was able to do; and Joshua was one of his chosen friends. We were both present at the sitting where he vowed, in answer to a taunt flung like a bomb-shell among the members, not to survive the insurrection. The effect was electrical; it was like a leaf out of old-world history, telling of a time when patriotism was a passion of which men were not ashamed. And when that noble old man rose so quietly, so solemnly, with no theatrical display or frothy excitement, but calmly registered the vow he afterwards kept with such sublime courage, it was as a torch that lighted every heart and soul there with Pentecostal fire. All knew what his words meant; and we, who shared his private thoughts and feelings as brothers, knew perhaps more than some others. Ah! the Society that needs such victims as Delescluze to bolster up its rottenness had better crumble to dust as it stands.

CHAPTER XII.

It was early in the evening, and we were walking slowly along the Boulevard Montmartre, when I saw a wayworn woman coming with staggering steps towards us, but at some distance yet. Her dress was torn ; her pale face was turned anxiously to each passer-by, scanning every one with a wild scrutiny, not curious so much as full of yearning ; her fair hair was hanging in disordered masses about her face and neck ; but when I tried to speak, pointing her out to Joshua, something in my throat prevented me. There was no need to speak ; she saw us almost as soon as I had recognised her, and, holding out her hands, as we came up hurriedly, said with a plaintive kind of weary smile, "I knew that I should light on you, Joshua!"

Then she sank in a heap at his feet, her arms stretched out, and her fair hair trailed in the dust.

Poor loving, faithful Mary! She had travelled for the last days on foot; and if we men had suffered on our journey, she had suffered ten times more. It seems she had set out almost immediately after us, though she had been more than three weeks longer on the road. She was but an ignorant girl, it must be remembered; she had not come yet to the point of knowing that obedience was even a higher quality than love, and that love is best shown by obedience

Here she was however, and we took her home to our lodgings in the Rue Blanche; and the concierge laughed significantly when asked for a room where she might be lodged. It would have been better to have refused her admission altogether, than to have laughed and leered as he did. The blood came into Joshua's pale face for just a moment; but there was no likelihood of his failing to do right for fear of its looking like wrong, so he gravely gave Mary his hand, and led her to our apartment. She was full of self-reproach and contrition when she saw the false position in which she had placed him; but he would not hear a word. "If you have been less than wise, my girl," he said, "you have been true of heart; so we will balance the one against the other, and cry quits!"

This concierge was a man who, from the first, inspired me with disgust and a vague dread. He was a red-haired, coarse-featured, ruffianly-looking fellow, by name Legros; now in the time of the Commune a noisy republican; but one could fancy him under the Empire standing with his greasy cap in hand shouting, "Vive l'Empereur!" with the loudest. He was a man who had not, I should say, one single guiding principle of life save selfishness—a frank, cynical, unabashed selfishness—a selfishness that believed in nothing save self; and to whom amassing miserable little sums of money to be spent in sensuality, was the ultimate of human cleverness and happiness; a man without faith, honour, justice, or mercy. I do not think I am too hard in my judgment of him; for he was one of the men

who make the theory of the devil very easy
to believe.

Among the sentiments professed by
Legros was that of disbelief in womanly
virtue. He laughed at the idea of purity
as possible in the friendship of men and women, and of course had his own ideas about
Mary; which it seems he expressed pretty
plainly. It was some gross insult, I never
heard precisely what, that he offered to the
poor girl which brought the whole thing to a
conclusion. We had both been out, leaving
her at home; and when we came back we
found her in a state of excitement and in-
dignation at something that had happened
during our absence. She told Joshua, not
me; and indeed, the first I rightly heard of
it was when Joshua came back from downstairs, where he had been into the porter's

lodge, and had thrashed Legros to within an inch of his life. This was the first and only time he had ever raised his hand against any one; and I was sorry he had not left the job to me. I would have done it as well, and he would have kept his hands clean. Yet for all this, when Legros, who had been wounded by a chance splinter, was in the hospital, Joshua attended to him specially, and mainly kept him alive by his care.

No one worked harder in these days of dread and turmoil than Joshua. This was what he had come to do. Among the poor and starving, the wounded and dismayed, there he was, day after day, helping all who needed so far as he could, tender as a woman, faithful and strong as a hero. Or he did the work of the Commune, as he might be ordered; and they had no more trustworthy official. Never a thought of self came in to weaken or distract him. For several nights at a stretch he did not go to bed, and he seemed to have the strength of half-a-dozen men, and to be kept up by an almost supernatural power. For the famine that was wasting the city was touching him with no tender hand. Day by day he got paler and thinner; his eyes, always bright and as if they were looking at something farther off than we could see, were sunk and dark and hollow; his cheeks were drawn and pale, his lips blackening and parched. But he never complained; he never seemed to think of himself at all; and if he had been without food for twelve hours or twenty-four, the chances were that he would share his scanty rations with the first passer-by who looked famine-stricken. Mary too was suffering from the want and privation of all kinds with which we were afflicted. We did what we could for her, be sure. If my life could have bought hers or his, I would have laid it down as willingly as I would have given them my bitter crust. But they bore up bravely, both of them; and she helped too with the sick and wounded. She was let to nurse in the English ambulances, where she was interpreted when necessary; and even at the worst her face as she went softly about the beds was pleasant for the sick and dying to look at. And here let me say how entirely in these late years all trace of her former condition had passed out of it. Purified by love; that was it; so that she looked now as if she might have come out of a convent. This is no fancy of my own. Any one who knew Joshua, and consequently

Mary Prinsep whom he had saved, will endorse what I say.

Things were looking wild and stormy, and the day of our doom was coming near. The Versaillists were too strong for us, and the hope of European freedom was over for the time; only for the time! For so sure as day follows on the night, so surely will the law of human rights follow on the tyrannies and oppressions which have so long ruled the world; and the faith for which the Commune bled, will be triumphant. But for the present, God help this poor sorrowful world of ours!

The Vicaire-Général had gone to Versailles, but he had not returned; and no answer had been vouchsafed to the offer made, now I think for the third time, to release the Archbishop and the other hostages for the one exchange of Blanqui. How often must the story be told? And will it ever be acknowledged by those who care only, right or wrong, to fasten the stain of blood-guiltiness on the Commune, that the real murderer of Monseigneur Darboy, and the rest, was M. Thiers? He knew what would happen, as well as a man knows what will happen if he puts a lighted match to a barrel of gunpowder. He knew that the hostages would be sacrificed. Inflamed as Paris was, surrounded by an enemy that treated her like a wild beast, and even shook hands with the common foe for her destruction, her best men spoken of as creatures below humanity, her hour of humiliation and bloody agony at hand— he knew there would be no calm reasoning out of consequences, no quiet acceptance of the result. Men's blood was up; and the result was foreseen and played for. It was a heavy stake to pay; but to discredit the Commune, and attach to it the ineffaceable stain of blood-guiltiness, was worth even an Archbishop and some sixty other lives !

We were at the prison during the time of the execution. It would be impossible to describe distinctly how it all took place. No one has, and no one ever will. The whole thing was confusion. No person knew exactly what was being done, or by whom; and no one had any recognised authority. The leaders of the Commune were fighting singly at the barricades, and for the time all executive government was at an end. The tumult and excitement at the prison was beyond all power of description. Men went and came; orders were given and contradicted ; women shrieked, some for blood and some for mercy; youths shouted; and through all, and above all, we heard the roar of the cannon, the whistling of the shells, and saw the smoke and flame of Paris rising up against the sky.

Joshua, mounted on a gun-barrel, pleaded for the lives of the unfortunate men.

"The work that the Commune had pledged itself to do," he said, "was to help on the freedom of the working classes, by proving to the world their nobility and power of self-government. The slaughter of unarmed men would do none of this. It would give their enemies a just handle against them, for it was a baseness unworthy of them—an act neither human nor noble, neither righteous nor generous. Whatever the wrong committed by the Government at Versailles, the innocent ought not to suffer. Let the Commune show itself supreme in virtue at this moment of trial, and put the temptation of blood-guiltiness away from it."

While he spoke Legros drew his revolver from his belt.

"Death to the English traitor!" he cried. "Death to the tool of the priests! he believes in Jesus Christ!"

"Christ! we want no Christs here? Death to the traitor!" shouted one or two of the mob.

Sick with dread for the safety of the man I loved best on earth, I sprang forward and covered Joshua's body with my own; when a fine-looking man—he was one of us then, but, as he is now in office under Thiers, I will not say who he was—quietly struck the revolver from Legros's hand.

"Keep your bullets for your enemies,

fool!—do not give them to your friends," he said; "this man is not a hostage." Then hurriedly, aside, to Joshua, "Escape while you can; I will cover your retreat, and divert their attention."

"Oh, that I had the voice of a God to teach them wisdom!" cried Joshua.

"Pshaw mon ami!" said our friend, contemptuously. "Your best wisdom now is to save your own life—not to try and teach men anything."

"Out with you, spies, traitors, priest-ridden Tartuffes!—we want no sympathizers with tyranny here!" shouted an excited, half-mad looking man close to us. "Out with them, citoyens!"

And at the word half-a-dozen men and women, shrieking and gesticulating, laid hands on us and roughly thrust us out. I thought it fortunate we left with our lives, for indeed, the wild, surging crowd was in no mood for mercy just then ; and a couple of lives, more or less, were of small account at that moment. Howbeit, we were flung out with many a blow and bitter word ; and just as we were going through the gateway a loud yell burst forth, a volley was fired, and we knew that the policy of Versailles had triumphed.

A few Parisians—*not the Commune*—had fallen into the snare prepared for them ; and the blood was shed which was to cover Liberty with shame, **until men** can hear and learn the truth.

The last day came. The guns of our forts were silent ; the **men were** fighting in the streets, desperate, conquered, but not craven. The Versaillists were pouring in like wolves let loose; Paris was drenched with blood, and in flames. And then the cry of the *pétroleuses* went up like the fire that shot against the sky. What mattered it that it was a lie? It gave the Party of Order another reason, if they had wanted any, to excuse their lust of blood. It was their saturnalia, and they did not stint themselves. The arms, that had served them so ill against the Prussians, served them but too well against their countrymen; and the short hour of a nation's hope was at an end in the bloody-reprisals of brothers, that exceeded all we have ever heard or read of in a victorious foreign army.

I had been separated from my friends for more than twenty-four hours. The house where we had lodged was in flames; and when I went to seek information at a Communist friend's, De Lancy, I found a group of three by the concierge door—himself, his young wife, and a little daughter not two years old, lying as if asleep, save for the blood that was their bed. They had been bound together and shot. Not one, but hundreds and thousands of such cases stand recorded in the history of that terrible moment, when the victorious Versaillists marched into Paris, and society revenged itself on the men who had dared to dream of redressing its wrongs ; and among the terrible sights that met me, the evidences of brutal, wanton, sickening murder, I had a shuddering dread that I should find Joshua and Mary. I was never so nearly mad as I was that day when I wandered about the bloody streets of Paris, looking for my friends ; sorrow for the lost cause, horror at the scenes I encountered, and fear for those I loved, all combining to render life in that hour simply torture.

At last I caught a glimpse of Mary crossing the street, carrying a wounded child in her arms, and making for the ambulance. I called to her, and hurried after her; but, weak as I was with excitement and want of food, I could not make my voice reach her.

Just then, cap in hand and bowing low, Jacques Legros rushed out of a ruined house and stopped the captain of a troop that came marching down the street. He pointed in a frantic way to Mary.

"V'la, mon Capitaine," he said, weeping and sobbing loudly, as one in the greatest distress; "c'est la cocotte d'un Communiste Anglais—c'est une pétroleuse! Elle a fait sauter la maison de ma mère. C'est ce que je sais, moi!"

"Prends-la," said the Captain in an odd, half bitter, half matter-of-fact way. And Mary was seized by a couple of his men, and brought up close to where he stood.

"C'est une jolie cible, ça!" he said with a brutal laugh. "C'est dommage—une belle fille comme ça! Mais on ne doit pas être pétroleuse, ma fille. Fi donc!"

"I have done no harm," said Mary, with her wild eyes searching his in vain for pity. "I have done only what good I could to all!"

"Is setting fire to honest women's houses doing good, wretch?" said the Captain, suddenly changing his mocking manner for one of ferocious sternness, and speaking in broken English. " A pétroleuse ?—you are not fit to live ! "

" She is no pétroleuse," I cried.

But as I spoke a blow laid me senseless ; and when I came to myself I found myself lying wounded on the ground, with Mary stretched beside me — shot through the heart.

It was then night time ; but soon after I recovered, and just as I was in the first agony of understanding what had happened, Joshua, and the same man who had saved his life at the time of the murder of the hostages in the prison, came up to where we lay, searching for us.

I have no more to tell of this episode Our Mary was buried tenderly, lovingly ; and I laid part of my life in her grave What Joshua felt I never knew exactly

He did not say much ; and though once I saw him, when he thought I was asleep, lay his head on his hands and weep bitterly, he never gave me a hint as to whether he was grieving at the loss of Mary, or at the failure of the cause. Whichever it was, it nearly broke him down ; and ill as I was myself, with a bad wound and a smashed collar-bone, I saw that his distress was greater than my own, and needed more consideration. I was desperately afraid more than once that he was going to die. For myself, I felt as if I could not die while Joshua lived, perhaps to want me.

However that might be, we neither of us came to grief of that kind. I got well in time ; and when I could travel, and a fitting opportunity arrived, our friend, who had kept us all this time in safety, got us sent off to

England.   And right glad was I when we landed safe in the Old Country once more. Joshua was glad too.   He had suffered much from the confinement, inertia, and disappointment of the last few weeks ;— coming too, after a time of such intense hope and excitement ; and once in England, he thought he could do something for the Humanity he loved, for the Truth to which he had consecrated **his life.**

CHAPTER XIII.

WE found times hard on our return. As for work, it was simply impossible to be had where we were known. If Joshua was shunned as a consorter with bad characters when he took vicious humanity by the hand, and sought to cleanse the foul and raise the degraded by the practical application of Christian precepts unsupported by sectarian organisation, what was he now, when besmirched with the Communistic doctrines of liberty, equality, and fraternity? Ordinary men thinking ordinary thoughts shrank from him in moral horror. He stood before them as the embodiment of murder and rapine, the representative of social destruction and the godless license of anarchy. He was a Communist: and that to most men and women of the day, means one wilfully and willingly guilty of every crime under heaven.

"They must be told the truth, John," he said to me one day; "whether they will accept it or not rests with themselves. But the work has to be done, and I have to do it, let what will be the result."

"It will be a bad one for you, Joshua," I said.

"So be it, my son. Preaching the Gospel brought most of the apostles to a bad end— as the world counts endings; and I am only following in their steps. I have got my Gospel to preach: the same our Master taught, if we could but get the world to see it!"

But that was just what neither he nor any one else has yet got the world to do, and I doubt it will be long before they will.

Work at the bench being impossible, being indeed scarcely the thing he wanted at this moment, Joshua took up again the hungry trade of political lecturer to working men, and went about the country explaining the Communistic doctrines, and showing their apostolic origin. His position was this. He did not justify all the actions of all the men at the head of affairs during the short reign of the Commune in Paris; but he warmly defended the cardinal points of their creed, as the logical outcome of Christianity in politics. The abolition of priestly supremacy in a man's social and daily life; the rights of labour as equal with those of capital; the dignity of humanity, including the doctrine of human equality; fraternal care for the poor, and the obligation laid on the strong to help the weak; the merely experimental nature of society, whence follows the righteousness of radical changes which shall break down the strongholds of tyranny and injustice, and help on general amelioration; the iniquity of maintaining the vested rights of wrong; and the right of the people to self-government. These were the doctrines he preached; but which he failed to induce the world to accept. They called him—as he called himself—a Communist; and the name offended, so that they would not listen to any kind of statement.

" You burnt Paris," said one. " You murdered innocent men," said another. "You insulted God and religion," said a third. A fourth—"You outraged morality, and lived in the most hideous licentiousness." "You would take our hard-earned savings from us, and reduce all men to one level—the idle with the industrious, and the ignorant with the educated," said a fifth. "You would rob the capitalist, and by so doing destroy the very labour you uphold," said a sixth.

And when he answered—"You mistake; I give up the blunders of the Commune, and the wrong-doing of which some of its members were guilty, only suggesting that they did not do all that was said of them; as neither did the early Christians slaughter children for their Eucharist, nor indulge in gross sin in their love feasts, as the Jews

said of them; but I maintain the doctrine.
Let me set that clearly before you, and I
will leave the rest to time and God "—as
often as not they turned against him, and
hounded him out of their towns.

"We want none of your French atheism
here," they said, when they were religiously
inclined; — "None of your Red-republi-
canism " when they were conservative.

But where parties were anything like even
enough to get him a handful of sympathizers,
there was generally a fight; and then the
magistrates ordered him out of the place,
with insult from the bench; and in many
towns they refused him permission to speak
at all. The very name of the Commune is
the red rag to English thought; and all
reason is lost when it is the question of
telling the truth about men who tried to get

the working classes equal rights and recognition with the moneyed ones.

At last we came to a place called Lowbridge, where a friend of ours lived—a
member of the International; and here
Joshua announced himself to give a lecture
on Communism, in the Town Hall. His programme stated the usual thing, that he,
Joshua Davidson, would show how Christ
and his apostles were Communists, and how
they preached the same doctrines which the
Commune of Paris strove to embody; allowing for the differences of method inherent
to the differences of social arrangements
that have grown up during a lapse of nearly
two thousand years.

The evening came, and Joshua prepared
to go to the meeting he had called; and
I along with him. Our friend had warned

him to expect an unfriendly audience; but Joshua was not a man to be daunted by a few stern faces; and I do not think I ever saw him so possessed with the spirit of what he had set out to teach as he was this evening. Yet also I noticed something in him that was not exactly like himself. Grave as he always was, to-night he was grave to sadness; a solemn kind of sadness; like a martyr going to his death, steadfast, testifying always, but—knowing that he was to die.

He shook hands with me at the side door cordially before going up, saying, "God bless you, John, you have been a true friend to me;" then smiled at me; and, the moment having come, stepped on to the platform.

In the first row, right in front of him, was the former clergyman of Trevalga; him

we lads used to call behind his back,
" Mr. Grand," because of his pomposity and
haughtiness. He had lately been given the
rich living of Lowbridge, and one or two
stately appointments connected with the
Cathedral and such like. I do not know
what they were éxactly, but they had made
him a man of supreme importance, not only
in Lowbridge itself, but in all the neighbourhood round about.

I saw Joshua's face change as he caught
the clergyman's eye. It did not change to
cowardice, but to a kind of eager look, like
a man taking hold of an enemy; and then
it passed away into his usual abstracted
unconsciousness of self, as he came quietly
to the front and prepared to speak. But
at the first word there broke out such a
tumult as I had never heard in any public

meeting, and I have been at a few rough
and rowdy ones too. The yells, hisses, cat-
calls, whoopings were indescribable. It
was impossible to be heard. I believe the
roar of a lion would have been overpowered.
Joshua stood there quiet and dignified as
ever, looking straight in among them, waiting for the tumult to cease. It only ceased
when Mr. Grand rose, and standing up on
the chair on which he had been sitting,
waved his hand for silence.

"Friends," he said, "I am glad that by
your honest English love of law and God,
you have shown what you think of the
poison this demagogue would have poured
into your ears. I know that man well,"
pointing to Joshua; "I have known him
from a boy; and I can bear my testimony to
the fact that he has been an ill-conditioned,

presumptuous, insolent fellow from the first. I know that he has led an infamous life in London ; and that he kept such a disorderly house the police were obliged to interfere ; and he was imprisoned for the offence. Loose women, thieves, burglars—all the scum of the earth have been his chosen companions ; and, to crown all, he went over to Paris at that awful time of the Commune, when, if ever hell was let loose on earth it was then, and joined himself to that band of miscreants who disgraced the very name of humanity. And now he has the audacity to come before you, honest and sober men of Lowbridge, loving your queen and country, abiding by the laws, and fearing God as I hope you all do. And what for ?—to praise that pandemonium of vice and crime—the Paris Commune — and blasphemously to liken those fiends in human shape to our Lord and the holy apostles ; to incite you to a rebellion as bloody as that ; and more than all this—to pick your pockets of your honest wages, that he, an idle vagabond, who won't work, may wander about the country, sowing his poison everywhere, while living on the fat of the land. Give him your minds, my men ; and let him understand that Lowbridge is not the place for a godless rascal like him at any time—and by no means the place for an atheist and a Communist!"

Then he got down, and the men cheered him as lustily as they had hissed Joshua.

I will do Mr. Grand the justice to say that I do not think he intended his words should have the effect they did have. Gentlefolks do not often incite to riot ; and a clergyman does not like to be the wirepuller for a murder. But, maddened by their own misconceptions to begin with, and excited still more by their parson's abuse and encouragement to violence as it were, the audience lost all self-control. A dozen men leaped on the platform, and in a moment I saw Joshua under their feet. It was in vain then for Mr. Grand to cry " Order "—for the two policemen at the doors to be sent for—for me to lay about me as hard as I was handled. The men had it all their own way. They were the representatives of law and order in their own minds, the champions of God and religion, and they regarded it as a sacred duty to take it out of this godless anarchist. Beaten, kicked, held back by a dozen or more, I could not help him. They beat me first ; and then the police beat me, and knocked me about savagely with their truncheons, because I struggled to get free, and to get to Joshua. He was lying on the ground, pale and senseless, with a stream of blood slowly flowing from his lips; while the men trampled on him and kicked him, and one, with a fearful oath, kicked him twice on the head. Suddenly a whisper ran round them, and they all drew a little way off; when, at a sign from one of them, the gas was turned down, and the place cleared as if by magic. When the lights were up again, and I went to lift him—he was dead.

I know no more—no more than this, that the man who had lived the life after Christ more exactly than any human being ever known to me, who had given himself to humanity and poured out his strength like water for the sacred cause, who had been loving, tolerant, pitiful to all—that man was killed by the Christian Party of Order; his memory denounced on the one hand as that of a blood-thirsty revolutionist who was justly punished for his crimes, on the other, as that of a presumptuous and heretical enthusiast who had insulted God and dishonoured the true faith. But the same things were said of the early Christians as have been said of him, of the Communists, and of all reformers of all times.

The world has ever disowned its Best when they came; and every truth has been planted in blood, and its first efforts sought to be checked by lies. So let them rest, our martyrs whom men do not yet know; as neither did they know eighteen hundred years ago the crucified Communist of Galilee—he who dwelt with lepers, made his friends of sinners, and preached against all the conventional respectabilities which society then held in honour.

The death of my friend has left me not only desolate, but uncertain. For I have come round to the old starting-point again : Is the Christian world all wrong, or is practical Christianity impossible? I see men simply and sincerely devoted to the cause of Humanity, and I hear the world's verdict on them. I hear others, earnest for the dogma of Christianity, rabid against its acted doctrines. They do not care to destroy the causes of misery by any change in social relations; they only attack the sinners for whose sin society is originally responsible. They maintain the unrighteous distinctions of caste as a religion; and they denounce as delusion, or impiety, the doctrine of universal brotherhood which Christ and His apostles preached and died for. I hear a great deal about faith, and the infidel being an accursed thing; but then I see the practical Christian, like Joshua, held accursed too. What does it all mean ? Let us have something definite. If the doctrines of Political Economy are true, if the law of the struggle for existence and the survival of the fittest applies absolutely to human society as well as to plants and fishes, let us then be frank, and candidly admit that Christianity, in its help to the poor and weak and in its patience with the sinner, is a craze; and let us abolish the pretence of a faith which influences neither our political institutions nor our social arrangements; and which ought not to influence them. If Christ was right, modern Christianity is wrong; but if sociology is a scientific truth, then Jesus of Nazareth preached and practised not only in vain, but against unchangeable Law.

Like Joshua in early days, my heart burns within me and my mind is unpiloted and unanchored. I cannot, being a Christian, accept the inhumanity of political economy and the obliteration of the individual in averages; yet I cannot reconcile modern science with Christ. Everywhere I see the sifting of competition, and nowhere Christian protection of weakness; everywhere dogma adored, and nowhere Christ realised. And again I ask, Which is true— modern society in its class strife and consequent elimination of its weaker erements,

or the brotherhood and communism taught
by the Jewish carpenter of Nazareth ? Who
will answer me ?—who will make the dark
thing clear ?

THE END.

PRINTED BY BALLANTYNE, HANSON AND CO.
LONDON AND EDINBURGH

CHEAP EDITIONS OF POPULAR NOVELS.

Post 8vo, illustrated boards, 2s. each.

By EDMOND ABOUT.
The Fellah.

By HAMILTON AÏDÉ.
Carr of Carrlyon. | Confidences.

By Mrs. ALEXANDER.
Maid, Wife, or Widow?

By SHELSLEY BEAUCHAMP.
Grantley Grange.

By BESANT AND RICE.
Ready-MoneyMortiboy. | Monks of Thelema.
WithHarp & Crown | 'Twas in Trafalgar's Bay.
This Son of Vulcan. | The Seamy Side.
My Little Girl. | Ten Years' Tenant.
Case of Mr. Lucraft | Chaplain of the
Golden Butterfly. | Fleet.
By Celia's Arbour. |

By FREDERICK BOYLE.
Camp Notes. | Savage Life.

By BRET HARTE.
An Heiress of Red Dog. | Gabriel Conroy
Luck of Roaring Camp. | Flip.

By ROBERT BUCHANAN.
The Shadow of the Sword.
A Child of Nature.

By Mrs. BURNETT.
Surly Tim.

By Mrs. LOVETT CAMERON.
Deceivers Ever. | Juliet's Guardian.

By MACLAREN COBBAN.
The Cure of Souls.

By C. ALLSTON COLLINS.
The Bar Sinister.

By WILKIE COLLINS.
Antonina. | Miss or Mrs.?
Basil. | The New Magdalen
Hide and Seek. | The Frozen Deep.
The Dead Secret. | TheLaw & theLady
Queen of Hearts. | The Two Destinies.
My Miscellanies. | The Haunted Hotel.
Woman in White. | The Fallen Leaves.
The Moonstone. | Jezebel's Daughter
Man and Wife | The Black Robe.
Poor Miss Finch. |

By MORTIMER COLLINS.
Sweet Anne Page. | Transmigration.
From Midnight to Midnight.
A Fight with Fortune.

By MORTIMER and FRANCES COLLINS.
Sweet & Twenty. | TheVillageComedy
Frances. | You Play me False.
Blacksmith and Scholar.

By DUTTON COOK.
Leo. | Paul Foster's Daughter.

By J. LEITH DERWENT.
Our Lady of Tears.

By CHARLES DICKENS.
Sketches by Boz. | Oliver Twist.
Pickwick Papers. | Nicholas Nickleby.

By Mrs. ANNIE EDWARDES.
A Point of Honour. | Archie Lovell.

By M. BETHAM-EDWARDS.
Felicia.

By EDWARD EGGLESTON.
Roxy.

By PERCY FITZGERALD.
Bella Donna. | Never Forgotten.
The Second Mrs. Tillotson.
Polly.
Seventy-five Brooke Street.

By ALBANY DE FONBLANQUE.
Filthy Lucro.

By R. E. FRANCILLON.
Olympia. | Queen Cophetua.
One by One.

By EDWARD GARRETT.
The Capel Girls.

By CHARLES GIBBON.
Robin Gray. | In Love and War.
For Lack of Gold. | For the King.
What will the | Queen of the Meadow.
World Say? | In Pastures Green.
In Honour Bound. |
The Dead Heart.

By WILLIAM GILBERT.
Dr. Austin's Guests.
The Wizard of the Mountain.
James Duke.

By JAMES GREENWOOD.
Dick Temple.

By ANDREW HALLIDAY.
Every-Day Papers.

By Lady DUFFUS HARDY.
Paul Wynter's Sacrifice.

By THOMAS HARDY.
Under the Greenwood Tree.

By JULIAN HAWTHORNE.
Garth. | Ellice Quentin.
Sebastian Strome.

By Sir ARTHUR HELPS.
Ivan de Biron.

By TOM HOOD.
A Golden Heart.

By VICTOR HUGO.
The Hunchback of Notre Dame.

By Mrs. ALFRED HUNT.
Thornicroft's Model. | Leaden Casket.

By JEAN INGELOW.
Fated to be Free.

By HENRY JAMES, Jun.
Confidence.

By HARRIETT JAY.
Dark Colleen. | Queen of Connaught.

By HENRY KINGSLEY.
Oakshott Castle. | Number Seventeen.

CHEAP EDITIONS OF POPULAR NOVELS.

Post 8vo, illustrated boards, 2s. each.

By E. LYNN LINTON.
Patricia Kemball. | With a Silken Thread.
The Atonement of Leam Dundas. | The Rebel of the Family.
World Well Lost. | "My Love!"
Under which Lord? |

By JUSTIN McCARTHY, M.P.
Dear Lady Disdain. | A Fair Saxon.
Waterdale Neighbours. [ter. | Linley Rochford.
My Enemy's Daugh- | Miss Misanthrope.
| Donna Quixote.

By GEORGE MACDONALD.
Paul Faber, Surgeon.
Thomas Wingfold, Curate.

By Mrs. MACDONELL.
Quaker Cousins.

By KATHARINE S. MACQUOID.
The Evil Eye. | Lost Rose.

By W. H. MALLOCK.
The New Republic.

By FLORENCE MARRYAT.
Open! Sesame! | Fighting the Air.
Harvest of Wild Oats | Written in Fire.
A Little Stepson. |

By JEAN MIDDLEMASS.
Touch and Go. | Mr. Dorillion.

By D. CHRISTIE MURRAY.
A Life's Atonement. | A Model Father.

By Mrs. OLIPHANT.
Whiteladies.

By Mrs. ROBERT O'REILLY.
Phœbe's Fortunes.

By OUIDA.
Held in Bondage. | Pascarel.
Strathmore. | Two Little Wooden Shoes.
Chandos. |
Under Two Flags. | Signa.
Idalia. | In a Winter City.
Cecil Castlemaine. | Ariadne.
Tricotrin. | Friendship.
Puck. | Moths.
Folle Farine. | Pipistrello.
A Dog of Flanders. | A Village Commune

By JAMES PAYN.
Lost Sir Massing- | Halves.
berd. | Fallen Fortunes.
A Perfect Treasure | What He Cost Her.
Bentinck's Tutor. | Humorous Stories.
Murphy's Master. | Gwendoline's Harvest. [Son.
A County Family. | Like Father, Like
At Her Mercy. | A Marine Residence. [Him.
A Woman's Vengeance. | Married Beneath
Cecil's Tryst. | Mirk Abbey.
Clyffards of Clyffe. | Not Wooed, but Won.
Family Scapegrace | £200 Reward.
Foster Brothers. | Less Black than
Found Dead. | We're Painted.
Best of Husbands. |
Walter's Word. |

By JAMES PAYN—continued.
By Proxy. | A Confidential Agent.
Under One Roof. |
High Spirits. | Some Private Views
Carlyon's Year. | From Exile.

By EDGAR A. POE.
The Mystery of Marie Roget.

By E. C. PRICE.
Valentina.

By CHARLES READE.
It is Never too Late to Mend. | Foul Play.
Hard Cash. | The Cloister and the Hearth.
Peg Woffington. | Course of True Love
Christie Johnstone | Autobiography of
Griffith Gaunt. | a Thief. [tion.
Put Yourself in His Place. | A Terrible Tempta-
| Wandering Heir.
Double Marriage. | A Simpleton.
Love Me Little, | A Woman-Hater.
Love Me Long. | Readiana.

By Mrs. RIDDELL.
Her Mother's Darling.

By BAYLE ST. JOHN.
A Levantine Family.

By GEORGE AUGUSTUS SALA.
Gaslight and Daylight.

By JOHN SAUNDERS.
Bound to the Wheel. | Guy Waterman.
One Against the World. | Lion in the Path.
| Two Dreamers.

By ARTHUR SKETCHLEY.
A Match in the Dark.

By T. W. SPEIGHT.
The Mysteries of Heron Dyke.

By R. A. STERNDALE.
The Afghan Knife.

By BERTHA THOMAS.
Cressida. | Proud Maisie.
The Violin-Player.

By WALTER THORNBURY.
Tales for the Marines.

By T. ADOLPHUS TROLLOPE.
Diamond Cut Diamond.

By ANTHONY TROLLOPE.
Way We Live Now. | American Senator

By MARK TWAIN.
Tom Sawyer. | An Idle Excursion.
A Pleasure Trip on the Continent of Europe.

By SARAH TYTLER.
What She Came Through.

By Lady WOOD.
Sabina.

By EDMUND YATES.
Castaway. | The Forlorn Hope.
Land at Last.

ANONYMOUS.
Paul Ferroll.
Why Paul Ferroll Killed his Wife.

CHATTO & WINDUS'S
LIST OF BOOKS.

*   *   *   *   *   *   *   *   *   *   *   *   *   *

About.—The Fellah: An Egyptian Novel. By EDMOND ABOUT. Translated by Sir RANDAL ROBERTS. Post 8vo, illustrated boards, 2s. ; cloth limp, 2s. 6d.

Adams (W. Davenport), Works by:

A Dictionary of the Drama. Being a comprehensive Guide to the Plays, Playwrights, Players, and Playhouses of the United Kingdom and America, from the Earliest to the Present Times. Crown 8vo, half-bound, 12s. 6d.   [*Preparing.*

Latter-Day Lyrics. Edited by W. DAVENPORT ADAMS. Post 8vo, cloth limp, 2s. 6d.

Quips and Quiddities. Selected by W. DAVENPORT ADAMS. Post 8vo, cloth limp, 2s. 6d.

Advertising, A History of, from the Earliest Times. Illustrated by Anecdotes, Curious Specimens, and Notices of Successful Advertisers. By HENRY SAMPSON. Crown 8vo, with Coloured Frontispiece and Illustrations, cloth gilt, 7s. 6d.

Agony Column (The) of "The Times," from 1800 to 1870. Edited, with an Introduction, by ALICE CLAY. Post 8vo, cloth limp, 2s. 6d.

Aide (Hamilton), Works by:
Carr of Carrlyon. Post 8vo, illustrated boards, 2s.

Confidences. Post 8vo, illustrated boards, 2s.

Alexander (Mrs.).—Maid, Wife, or Widow? A Romance. By Mrs. ALEXANDER. Post 8vo, illustrated boards, 2s. ; cr. 8vo, cloth extra, 3s 6d.

Allen (Grant), Works by:·

The Evolutionist at Large. Second Edition, revised. Cr. 8vo, cl. extra, 6s.

Vignettes from Nature. Crown 8vo, cloth extra, 6s.

Colin Clout's Calendar. Crown 8vo, cloth extra, 6s.

Architectural Styles, A Handbook of. Translated from the German of A. ROSENGARTEN, by W. COLLETT-SANDARS. Crown 8vo, cloth extra, with 639 Illustrations, 7s. 6d.

Art (The) of Amusing: A Collection of Graceful Arts, Games, Tricks, Puzzles, and Charades. By FRANK BELLEW. With 300 Illustrations. Cr. 8vo, cloth extra, 4s. 6d.

Artemus Ward :

Artemus Ward's Works: The Works of CHARLES FARRER BROWNE, better known as ARTEMUS WARD. With Portrait and Facsimile. Crown 8vo, cloth extra, 7s. 6d.

Artemus Ward's Lecture on the Mormons. With 32 Illustrations. Edited, with Preface, by EDWARD P. HINGSTON. Crown 8vo, 6d.

The Genial Showman: Life and Adventures of Artemus Ward. By EDWARD P. HINGSTON. With a Frontispiece. Crown 8vo, cloth extra, 3s. 6d.

Ashton (John), Works by:

A History of the Chap-Books of the Eighteenth Century. With nearly 400 Illusts., engraved in facsimile of the originals. Cr. 8vo, cl. ex., 7s. 6d.

Social Life in the Reign of Queen Anne. From Original Sources. With nearly 100 Illusts. Cr.8vo,cl.ex.,7s.6d.

Humour, Wit, and Satire of the Seventeenth Century. With nearly 100 Illusts. Cr. 8vo, cl. extra, 7s. 6d.

English Caricature and Satire on Napoleon the First. 120 Illusts. from Originals. Two Vols., demy 8vo, 28s.

Bacteria.—A Synopsis of the Bacteria and Yeast Fungi and Allied Species. By W. B. GROVE, B.A. With 87 Illusts. Crown 8vo, cl. extra, 3s. 6d.

Balzac's " Comedie Humaine " and its Author. With Translations by H. H. WALKER. Post 8vo, cl.limp.2s. 6d.

Bankers, A Handbook of Lon-don; together with Lists of Bankers from 1677. By F. G. HILTON PRICE. Crown 8vo, cloth extra, 7s. 6d.

Bardsley (Rev. C.W.),Works by:

English Surnames: Their Sources and Si nifications. Third Ed., revised. Cr. 8vo, cl. extra, 7s. 6d. [*Preparing.*

Curiosities of Puritan Nomenclature. Crown 8vo, cloth extra, 7s. 6d.

Bartholomew Fair, Memoirs of. By HENRY MORLEY. With 100 Illusts. Crown 8vo, cloth extra, 7s. 6d.

Basil, Novels by:

A Drawn Game. Three Vols., cr. 8vo.

The Wearing of the Green. Three Vols., crown 8vo.   [*Shortly.*

Beaconsfield, Lord: A Biography. By T. P. O'CONNOR, M.P. Sixth Edit., New Preface. Cr.8vo,cl.ex.7s.6d.

Beauchamp. — Grantley Grange: A Novel. By SHELSLEY BEAUCHAMP. Post 8vo, illust. bds., 2s.

Beautiful Pictures by British Artists: A Gathering of Favourites from our Picture Galleries. In Two Series. All engraved on Steel in the highest style of Art. Edited, with Notices of the Artists, by SYDNEY ARMYTAGE, M.A. Imperial 4to, cloth extra, gilt and gilt edges, 21s. per Vol.

Bechstein. — As Pretty as Seven, and other German Stories. Collected by LUDWIG BECHSTEIN. With Additional Tales by the Brothers GRIMM, and 100 Illusts. by RICHTER. Small 4to, green and gold, 6s. 6d.; Li'' ln c, 7s. 6d.

Beerbohm. — Wanderings in Patagonia; or, Life among the Ostrich Hunters. By JULIUS BEERBOHM. With Illusts. Crown 8vo, cloth extra, 3s. 6d.

Belgravia for 1884. One Shilling Monthly, Illustrated by P. MACNAB.—Two Serial Stories are now appearing in this Magazine: "The Lover's Creed," by Mrs. CASHEL HOEY; and " The Wearing of the Green," by the Author of " Love the Debt."

⁂ *Now ready, the Volume for* MARCH *to* JUNE, 1884, *cloth extra, gilt edges,* 7s. 6d.; *Cases for binding Vols.,* 2s. *each.*

Belgravia Annual. With Stories by F. W. ROBINSON, J. ARBUTHNOT WILSON, JUSTIN H. MCCARTHY, B. MONTGOMERIE RANKING, and others. Demy 8vo, with Illusts., 1s. [*Preparing.*

Bennett (W.C.,LL.D.),Works by:

A Ballad History of England. Post 8vo, cloth limp, 2s.

Songs for Sailors. Post 8vo, cloth limp, 2s.

Besant (Walter) and James Rice, Novels by. Post 8vo, illust. boards, 2s. each; cloth limp, 2s. 6d. each; or crown 8vo, cloth extra, 3s. 6d. each.

Ready-Money Mortiboy.

With Harp and Crown.

This Son of Vulcan.

My Little Girl.

The Case of Mr. Lucraft.

The Golden Butterfly.

By Celia's Arbour.

The Monks of Thelema.

'Twas In Trafalgar's Bay.

The Seamy Side.

The Ten Years' Tenant.

The Chaplain of the Fleet.

Besant (Walter), Novels by:

All Sorts and Conditions of Men: An Impossible Story. With Illustrations by FRED. BARNARD. Crown 8vo, cloth extra, 3s. 6d.; post 8vo, illust. boards, 2s.; cloth limp, 2s. 6d.

The Captains' Room, &c. With Frontispiece by E. J. WHEELER. Crown 8vo, cloth extra, 3s. 6d.; post 8vo, illust. bds., 2s.; cl. limp, 2s. 6d.

All In a Garden Fair. With 6 Illusts. by H. FURNISS. New and Cheaper Edition. Cr. 8vo, cl. extra, 3s. 6d.

Dorothy Forster. New and Cheaper Edition. With Illustrations by CH. GREEN. Crown 8vo, cloth extra, 3s. 6d. [*Preparing.*

The Art of Fiction. Demy 8vo, 1s.

Betham-Edwards (M.), Novels by. Crown 8vo, cloth extra, 3s. 6d. each.; post 8vo, illust. bds., 2s. each.

Felicia. | Kitty.

Bewick (Thos.) and his Pupils. By Austin Dobson. With 95 Illustrations. Square 8vo, cloth extra, 10s. 6d.

Birthday Books:—

The Starry Heavens: A Poetical Birthday Book. Square 8vo, handsomely bound in cloth, 2s. 6d.

Birthday Flowers: Their Language and Legends. By W. J. Gordon. Beautifully Illustrated in Colours by Viola Boughton. In illuminated cover, crown 4to, 6s.

The Lowell Birthday Book. With Illusts., small 8vo, cloth extra, 4s. 6d.

Blackburn's (Henry) Art Handbooks. Demy 8vo, Illustrated, uniform in size for binding.

Academy Notes, separate years, from 1875 to 1883, each 1s.

Academy Notes, 1884. With 152 Illustrations. 1s.

Academy Notes, 1875–79. Complete in One Vol., with nearly 600 Illusts. in Facsimile. Demy 8vo, cloth limp, 6s.

Academy Notes, 1880–84. Complete in One Volume, with about 700 Facsimile Illustrations. Cloth limp, 6s.

Grosvenor Notes, 1877. 6d.

Grosvenor Notes, separate years, from 1878 to 1883, each 1s.

Grosvenor Notes, 1884. With 73 Illustrations. 1s.

Grosvenor Notes, 1877–82. With upwards of 300 Illustrations. Demy 8vo, cloth limp, 6s.

Pictures at South Kensington. With 70 Illustrations. 1s.

The English Pictures at the National Gallery. 114 Illustrations. 1s.

The Old Masters at the National Gallery. 128 Illustrations. 1s. 6d.

A Complete Illustrated Catalogue to the National Gallery. With Notes by H. Blackburn, and 242 Illusts. Demy 8vo, cloth limp, 3s.

Illustrated Catalogue of the Luxembourg Gallery. Containing about 250 Reproductions after the Original Drawings of the Artists. Edited by F. G. Dumas. Demy 8vo, 3s. 6d,

The Paris Salon, 1884. With over 300 Illusts. Edited by F. G. Dumas. Demy 8vo, 3s,

Art Handbooks, *continued—*

The Art Annual, 1883–4. Edited by F. G. Dumas. With 300 full-page Illustrations. Demy 8vo, 5s.

Boccaccio's Decameron ; or, Ten Days' Entertainment. Translated into English, with an Introduction by Thomas Wright, F.S.A. With Portrait, and Stothard's beautiful Copperplates. Cr. 8vo, cloth extra, gilt, 7s. 6d.

Blake (William): Etchings from his Works. By W. B. Scott. With descriptive Text. Folio, half-bound boards, India Proofs, 21s.

Bowers'(G.) Hunting Sketches:

Canters in Crampshire. Oblong 4to, half-bound boards, 21s.

Leaves from a Hunting Journal. Coloured in facsimile of the originals. Oblong 4to, half-bound, 21s.

Boyle (Frederick), Works by:

Camp Notes: Stories of Sport and Adventure in Asia, Africa, and America. Crown 8vo, cloth extra, 3s. 6d.; post 8vo, illustrated bds., 2s.

Savage Life. Crown 8vo, cloth extra, 3s. 6d.; post 8vo, illustrated bds., 2s.

Brand's Observations on Popular Antiquities, chiefly Illustrating the Origin of our Vulgar Customs, Ceremonies, and Superstitions. With the Additions of Sir Henry Ellis. Crown 8vo, cloth extra, gilt, with numerous Illustrations, 7s. 6d.

Bret Harte, Works by:

Bret Harte's Collected Works. Arranged and Revised by the Author. Complete in Five Vols., crown 8vo, cloth extra, 6s. each.

   Vol. I. Complete Poetical and Dramatic Works. With Steel Portrait, and Introduction by Author.

   Vol. II. Earlier Papers—Luck of Roaring Camp, and other Sketches—Bohemian Papers — Spanish and American Legends.

   Vol. III. Tales of the Argonauts—Eastern Sketches.

   Vol. IV. Gabriel Conroy.

   Vol. V. Stories — Condensed Novels, &c.

The Select Works of Bret Harte, in Prose and Poetry. With Introductory Essay by J. M. Bellew, Portrait of the Author, and 50 Illustrations. Crown 8vo, cloth extra, 7s. 6d.

Gabriel Conroy: A Novel. Post 8vo, illustrated boards, 2s.

Bret Harte's Works, *continued*—

An Heiress of Red Dog, and other Stories. Post 8vo, illustrated boards, 2s.; cloth limp, 2s. 6d.

The Twins of Table Mountain. Fcap. 8vo, picture cover, 1s.; crown 8vo, cloth extra, 3s. 6d.

Luck of Roaring Camp, and other Sketches. Post 8vo, illust. bds., 2s.

Jeff Briggs's Love Story. Fcap. 8vo, picture cover, 1s.; cloth extra, 2s. 6d.

Flip. Post 8vo, illustrated boards, 2s.; cloth limp, 2s. 6d.

Californian Stories (including The Twins of Table Mountain, Jeff Briggs's Love Story. &c.) Post 8vo, illustrated boards, 2s.

Brewer (Rev. Dr.), Works by :

The Reader's Handbook of Allusions, References, Plots, and Stories. Fourth Edition, revised throughout, with a New Appendix, containing a Complete English Bibliography. Cr. 8vo, 1,400 pp., cloth extra, 7s. 6d.

Authors and their Works, with the Dates: Being the Appendices to "The Reader's Handbook," separately printed. Cr. 8vo, cloth limp, 2s.

A Dictionary of Miracles: Imitative, Realistic, and Dogmatic. Crown 8vo, cloth extra, 7s. 6d.; half-bound, 9s.

Brewster(Sir David), Works by :

More Worlds than One: The Creed of the Philosopher and the Hope of the Christian. With Plates. Post 8vo, cloth extra, 4s. 6d.

The Martyrs of Science: Lives of Galileo, Tycho Brahe, and Kepler. With Portraits. Post 8vo, cloth extra, 4s. 6d.

Letters on Natural Magic. A New Edition, with numerous Illustrations, and Chapters on the Being and Faculties of Man, and Additional Phenomena of Natural Magic, by J. A. Smith. Post 8vo, cloth extra, 4s. 6d.

Brillat-Savarin.—Gastronomy

as a Fine Art. By Brillat-Savarin. Translated by R. E. Anderson, M.A. Post 8vo, cloth limp, 2s. 6d.

Burnett (Mrs.), Novels by :

Surly Tim, and other Stories. Post 8vo, illustrated boards, 2s.

Kathleen Mavourneen. Fcap. 8vo, picture cover, 1s.

Lindsay's Luck. Fcap. 8vo, picture cover, 1s.

Pretty Polly Pemberton. Fcap. 8vo, picture cover, 1s.

Buchanan's (Robert) Works :

Ballads of Life, Love, and Humour. With a Frontispiece by Arthur Hughes. Crown 8vo, cloth extra, 6s.

Selected Poems of Robert Buchanan. With Frontispiece by T. Dalziel. Crown 8vo, cloth extra, 6s.

Undertones. Cr. 8vo, cloth extra, 6s.

London Poems. Cr. 8vo, cl. extra, 6s.

The Book of Orm. Crown 8vo, cloth extra, 6s.

White Rose and Red: A Love Story. Crown 8vo, cloth extra, 6s.

Idylls and Legends of Inverburn. Crown 8vo, cloth extra, 6s.

St. Abe and his Seven Wives : A Tale of Salt Lake City. With a Frontispiece by A. B. Houghton. Crown 8vo, cloth extra, 5s.

Robert Buchanan's Complete Poetical Works. With Steel-plate Portrait. Crown 8vo, cloth extra, 7s. 6d.   [*In the press.*

The Hebrid Isles: Wanderings in the Land of Lorne and the Outer Hebrides. With Frontispiece by W. Small. Crown 8vo, cloth extra, 6s.

A Poet's Sketch-Book: Selections from the Prose Writings of Robert Buchanan. Crown 8vo, cl. extra, 6s.

The Shadow of the Sword: A Romance. Crown 8vo, cloth extra, 3s. 6d.; post 8vo, illust. boards, 2s.

A Child of Nature: A Romance. With a Frontispiece. Crown 8vo, cloth extra, 3s. 6d.; post 8vo, illust. bds., 2s.

God and the Man: A Romance. With Illustrations by Fred. Barnard. Crown 8vo, cloth extra, 3s. 6d.; post 8vo, illustrated boards, 2s.

The Martyrdom of Madeline: A Romance. With Frontispiece by A. W. Cooper. Cr. 8vo, cloth extra, 3s. 6d.; post 8vo, illustrated boards, 2s.

Love Me for Ever. With a Frontispiece by P. Macnab. Crown 8vo, cloth extra, 3s. 6d.; post 8vo, illustrated boards, 2s.

Annan Water: A Romance. Crown 8vo, cloth extra, 3s. 6d.

The New Abelard: A Romance. Crown 8vo, cloth extra, 3s. 6d.

Foxglove Manor: A Novel. Three Vols., crown 8vo.

Burton (Robert):

The Anatomy of Melancholy. A New Edition, complete, corrected and enriched by Translations of the Classical Extracts. Demy 8vo, cloth extra, 7s. 6d.

Melancholy Anatomised: Being an Abridgment, for popular use, of Burton's Anatomy of Melancholy. Post 8vo, cloth limp, 2s. 6d.

Burton (Captain), Works by:

To the Gold Coast for Gold: A Personal Narrative. By RICHARD F. BURTON and VERNEY LOVETT CAMERON. With Maps and Frontispiece. Two Vols., crown 8vo, cloth extra, 21s.

The Book of the Sword: Being a History of the Sword and its Use in all Countries, from the Earliest Times. By RICHARD F. BURTON. With over 400 Illustrations. Square 8vo, cloth extra, 32s.

Bunyan's Pilgrim's Progress. Edited by Rev. T. SCOTT. With 17 Steel Plates by STOTHARD, engraved by GOODALL, and numerous Woodcuts. Crown 8vo, cloth extra, gilt, 7s. 6d.

Byron (Lord):

Byron's Letters and Journals. With Notices of his Life. By THOMAS MOORE. A Reprint of the Original Edition, newly revised, with Twelve full-page Plates. Crown 8vo, cloth extra, gilt, 7s. 6d.

Byron's Don Juan. Complete in One Vol., post 8vo, cloth limp, 2s.

Cameron (Commander) and Captain Burton.—To the Gold Coast for Gold: A Personal Narrative. By RICHARD F. BURTON and VERNEY LOVETT CAMERON. With Frontispiece and Maps. Two Vols., crown 8vo, cloth extra, 21s.

Cameron (Mrs. H. Lovett), Novels by:

Crown 8vo, cloth extra, 3s. 6d. each; post 8vo, illustrated boards, 2s. each.

Juliet's Guardian.

Deceivers Ever.

Campbell.—White and Black: Travels in the United States. By Sir GEORGE CAMPBELL, M.P. Demy 8vo, cloth extra, 14s.

Carlyle (Thomas):

Thomas Carlyle: Letters and Recollections. By MONCURE D. CONWAY, M.A. Crown 8vo, cloth extra, with Illustrations, 6s.

On the Choice of Books. By THOMAS CARLYLE. With a Life of the Author by R. H. SHEPHERD. New and Revised Edition, post 8vo, cloth extra, Illustrated, 1s. 6d.

The Correspondence of Thomas Carlyle and Ralph Waldo Emerson, 1834 to 1872. Edited by CHARLES ELIOT NORTON. With Portraits. Two Vols., crown 8vo, cloth extra, 24s.

Chapman's (George) Works: Vol. I. contains the Plays complete, including the doubtful ones. Vol. II., the Poems and Minor Translations, with an Introductory Essay by ALGERNON CHARLES SWINBURNE. Vol. III., the Translations of the Iliad and Odyssey. Three Vols., crown 8vo, cloth extra, 18s.; or separately, 6s. each.

Chatto & Jackson.—A Treatise on Wood Engraving, Historical and Practical. By WM. ANDREW CHATTO and JOHN JACKSON. With an Additional Chapter by HENRY G. BOHN; and 450 fine Illustrations. A Reprint of the last Revised Edition. Large 4to, half-bound, 28s.

Chaucer:

Chaucer for Children: A Golden Key. By Mrs. H. R. HAWEIS. With Eight Coloured Pictures and numerous Woodcuts by the Author. New Ed., small 4to, cloth extra, 6s.

Chaucer for Schools. By Mrs. H. R. HAWEIS. Demy 8vo, cloth limp, 2s.6d.

City (The) of Dream: A Poem. Fcap. 8vo, cloth extra, 6s. [*In the press.*

Cobban.—The Cure of Souls: A Story. By J. MACLAREN COBBAN. Post 8vo, illustrated boards, 2s.

Collins (C. Allston).—The Bar Sinister: A Story. By C. ALLSTON COLLINS. Post 8vo, illustrated bds.,2s.

Collins (Mortimer & Frances), Novels by:

Sweet and Twenty. Post 8vo, illustrated boards, 2s.

Frances. Post 8vo, illust. bds., 2s.

Blacksmith and Scholar. Post 8vo, illustrated boards, 2s.; crown 8vo, cloth extra, 3s. 6d.

The Village Comedy. Post 8vo, illust. boards, 2s.; cr. 8vo, cloth extra, 3s. 6d.

You Play Me False. Post 8vo, illust. boards, 2s.; cr. 8vo, cloth extra, 3s. 6d.

Collins (Mortimer), Novels by:

Sweet Anne Page. Post 8vo, illustrated boards, 2s.; crown 8vo, cloth extra, 3s. 6d.

Transmigration. Post 8vo, illustrated boards, 2s.; crown 8vo, cloth extra, 3s. 6d.

From Midnight to Midnight. Post 8vo, illustrated boards, 2s.; crown 8vo, cloth extra, 3s. 6d.

A Fight with Fortune. Post 8vo, illustrated boards, 2s.

Collins (Wilkie), Novels by.

Each post 8vo, illustrated boards, 2s; cloth limp, 2s. 6d.; or crown 8vo, cloth extra, Illustrated, 3s. 6d.

Antonina. Illust. by A. CONCANEN.

Basil. Illustrated by Sir JOHN GILBERT and J. MAHONEY.

Hide and Seek. Illustrated by Sir JOHN GILBERT and J. MAHONEY.

The Dead Secret. Illustrated by Sir JOHN GILBERT and A. CONCANEN.

Queen of Hearts Illustrated by Sir JOHN GILBERT and A. CONCANEN.

My Miscellanies. With Illustrations by A. CONCANEN, and a Steel-plate Portrait of WILKIE COLLINS.

The Woman in White. With Illustrations by Sir JOHN GILBERT and F. A. FRASER.

The Moonstone. With Illustrations by G. DU MAURIER and F. A. FRASER.

Man and Wife. Illust. by W. SMALL.

Poor Miss Finch. Illustrated by G. DU MAURIER and EDWARD HUGHES.

Miss or Mrs.? With Illustrations by S. L. FILDES and HENRY WOODS.

The New Magdalen. Illustrated by G. DU MAURIER and C. S. RANDS.

The Frozen Deep. Illustrated by G. DU MAURIER and J. MAHONEY.

The Law and the Lady. Illustrated by S. L. FILDES and SYDNEY HALL.

The Two Destinies.

The Haunted Hotel. Illustrated by ARTHUR HOPKINS.

The Fallen Leaves.

Jezebel's Daughter.

The Black Robe.

Heart and Science: A Story of the Present Time. Crown 8vo, cloth extra, 3s. 6d.

"I Say No." Three Vols., crown 8vo. [*Shortly.*

Colman's Humorous Works:

"Broad Grins," "My Nightgown and Slippers," and other Humorous Works, Prose and Poetical, of GEORGE COLMAN. With Life by G. B. BUCKSTONE, and Frontispiece by HOGARTH. Crown 8vo, cloth extra, gilt, 7s. 6d.

Convalescent Cookery: A

Family Handbook. By CATHERINE RYAN. Post 8vo, cloth limp, 2s. 6d.

Conway (Moncure D.), Works by:

Demonology and Devil-Lore. Two Vols., royal 8vo, with 65 Illusts., 28s.

CONWAY'S (M. D.) WORKS, *continued*—

A Necklace of Stories. Illustrated by W. J. HENNESSY. Square 8vo, cloth extra, 6s.

The Wandering Jew. Crown 8vo, cloth extra, 6s.

Thomas Carlyle: Letters and Recollections. With Illustrations. Crown 8vo, cloth extra, 6s.

Cook (Dutton), Works by:

Hours with the Players. With a Steel Plate Frontispiece. New and Cheaper Edit., cr. 8vo, cloth extra, 6s.

Nights at the Play: A View of the English Stage. New and Cheaper Edition. Crown 8vo, cloth extra, 6s.

Leo: A Novel. Post 8vo, illustrated boards, 2s.

Paul Foster's Daughter. Post 8vo, illustrated boards, 2s.; crown 8vo, cloth extra, 3s. 6d.

Cooper.—Heart Salvage, by

Sea and Land. Stories by Mrs. COOPER (KATHARINE SAUNDERS). Three Vols., crown 8vo.

Copyright. — A Handbook of

English and Foreign Copyright in Literary and Dramatic Works. By SIDNEY JERROLD, of the Middle Temple, Esq., Barrister-at-Law. Post 8vo, cloth limp, 2s. 6d.

Cornwall.—Popular Romances

of the West of England; or, The Drolls, Traditions, and Superstitions of Old Cornwall. Collected and Edited by ROBERT HUNT, F.R.S. New and Revised Edition, with Additions, and Two Steel-plate Illustrations by GEORGE CRUIKSHANK. Crown 8vo, cloth extra, 7s. 6d.

Creasy.—Memoirs of Eminent

Etonians: with Notices of the Early History of Eton College. By Sir EDWARD CREASY, Author of "The Fifteen Decisive Battles of the World." Crown 8vo, cloth extra, gilt, with 13 Portraits, 7s. 6d.

Cruikshank (George):

The Comic Almanack. Complete in TWO SERIES: The FIRST from 1835 to 1843; the SECOND from 1844 to 1853. A Gathering of the BEST HUMOUR of THACKERAY, HOOD, MAYHEW, ALBERT SMITH, A'BECKETT, ROBERT BROUGH, &c. With 2,000 Woodcuts and Steel Engravings by CRUIKSHANK, HINE, LANDELLS, &c. Crown 8vo, cloth gilt, two very thick volumes, 7s. 6d. each.

CRUIKSHANK (G.), *continued—*

The Life of George Cruikshank. By BLANCHARD JERROLD, Author of "The Life of Napoleon III.," &c. With 84 Illustrations. New and Cheaper Edition, enlarged, with Additional Plates, and a very carefully compiled Bibliography. Crown 8vo, cloth extra, 7s. 6d.

Robinson Crusoe. A beautiful reproduction of Major's Edition, with 37 Woodcuts and Two Steel Plates by GEORGE CRUIKSHANK, choicely printed. Crown 8vo, cloth extra, 7s. 6d. A few Large-Paper copies, printed on hand-made paper, with India proofs of the Illustrations, 36s.

Cussans.—Handbook of Heraldry; with Instructions for Tracing Pedigrees and Deciphering Ancient MSS., &c. By JOHN E. CUSSANS. Entirely New and Revised Edition, illustrated with over 400 Woodcuts and Coloured Plates. Crown 8vo, cloth extra, 7s. 6d.

Cyples.—Hearts of Gold: A Novel. By WILLIAM CYPLES. Crown 8vo, cloth extra, 3s. 6d.

Daniel. — Merrie England in the Olden Time. By GEORGE DANIEL. With Illustrations by ROBT. CRUIKSHANK. Crown 8vo, cloth extra, 3s. 6d.

Daudet.—Port Salvation; or, The Evangelist. By ALPHONSE DAUDET. Translated by C. HARRY MELTZER. With Portrait of the Author. Crown 8vo, cloth extra, 3s. 6d.

Davenant. — What shall my Son be? Hints for Parents on the Choice of a Profession or Trade for their Sons. By FRANCIS DAVENANT, M.A. Post 8vo, cloth limp, 2s. 6d.

Davies (Dr. N. E.), Works by:

One Thousand Medical Maxims. Crown 8vo, 1s.; cloth, 1s. 6d.

Nursery Hints: A Mother's Guide. Crown 8vo, 1s.; cloth, 1s. 6d.

Aids to Long Life. Crown 8vo, 2s.; cloth limp, 2s. 6d. [*Shortly.*

Davies' (Sir John) Complete Poetical Works, including Psalms I. to L. in Verse, and other hitherto Unpublished MSS., for the first time Collected and Edited, with Memorial-Introduction and Notes, by the Rev. A. B. GROSART, D.D. Two Vols., crown 8vo, cloth boards, 12s.

De Maistre.—A Journey Round My Room. By XAVIER DE MAISTRE. Translated by HENRY ATTWELL. Post 8vo, cloth limp, 2s. 6d.

De Mille.—A Castle in Spain. A Novel. By JAMES DE MILLE. With a Frontispiece. Crown 8vo, cloth extra, 3s. 6d.

Derwent (Leith), Novels by:

Our Lady of Tears. Cr. 8vo, cloth extra, 3s. 6d.; post 8vo, illust. bds., 2s.

Circe's Lovers. Crown 8vo, cloth extra, 3s. 6d.

Dickens (Charles), Novels by:

Post 8vo, illustrated boards, 2s. each.

Sketches by Boz. | Nicholas Nickleby.
Pickwick Papers. | Oliver Twist.

The Speeches of Charles Dickens. (*Mayfair Library.*) Post 8vo, cloth limp, 2s. 6d.

The Speeches of Charles Dickens, 1841-1870. With a New Bibliography, revised and enlarged. Edited and Prefaced by RICHARD HERNE SHEPHERD. Crown 8vo, cloth extra, 6s.

About England with Dickens. By ALFRED RIMMER. With 57 Illustrations by C. A. VANDERHOOF, ALFRED RIMMER, and others. Sq. 8vo, cloth extra, 10s. 6d.

Dictionaries:

A Dictionary of Miracles: Imitative, Realistic, and Dogmatic. By the Rev. E. C. BREWER, LL.D. Crown 8vo, cloth extra, 7s. 6d.; hf.-bound, 9s.

The Reader's Handbook of Allusions, References, Plots, and Stories. By the Rev. E. C. BREWER, LL.D. Fourth Edition, revised throughout, with a New Appendix, containing a Complete English Bibliography. Crown 8vo, 1,400 pages, cloth extra, 7s. 6d.

Authors and their Works, with the Dates. Being the Appendices to "The Reader's Handbook," separately printed. By the Rev. E. C. BREWER, LL.D. Crown 8vo, cloth limp, 2s.

Familiar Allusions: A Handbook of Miscellaneous Information; including the Names of Celebrated Statues, Paintings, Palaces, Country Seats, Ruins, Churches, Ships, Streets, Clubs, Natural Curiosities, and the like. By WM. A. WHEELER and CHARLES G. WHEELER. Demy 8vo cloth extra, 7s. 6d.

DICTIONARIES, *continued—*

Short Sayings of Great Men. With Historical and Explanatory Notes. By SAMUEL A. BENT, M.A. Demy 8vo, cloth extra, 7s. 6d.

A Dictionary of the Drama: Being a comprehensive Guide to the Plays, Playwrights, Players, and Playhouses of the United Kingdom and America, from the Earliest to the Present Times. By W. DAVENPORT ADAMS. A thick volume, crown 8vo, half-bound, 12s. 6d.   [*In preparation.*]

The Slang Dictionary: Etymological, Historical, and Anecdotal. Crown 8vo, cloth extra, 6s. 6d.

Words, Facts, and Phrases: A Dictionary of Curious, Quaint, and Out-of-the-Way Matters. By ELIEZER EDWARDS. New and Cheaper Issue. Cr. 8vo, cl. ex., 7s. 6d. ; hf.-bd., 9s.

Diderot.—The Paradox of Acting. Translated, with Annotations, from Diderot's "Le Paradoxe sur le Comédien," by WALTER HERRIES POLLOCK. With a Preface by HENRY IRVING. Cr. 8vo, in parchment, 4s. 6d.

Dobson (W. T.), Works by :

Literary Frivolities, Fancies, Follies, and Frolics. Post 8vo, cl. lp., 2s. 6d.

Poetical Ingenuities and Eccentricities. Post 8vo, cloth limp, 2s. 6d.

Doran. — Memories of our Great Towns; with Anecdotic Gleanings concerning their Worthies and their Oddities. By Dr. JOHN DORAN, F.S.A. With 38 Illustrations. New and Cheaper Ed., cr. 8vo, cl. ex., 7s. 6d.

Drama, A Dictionary of the. Being a comprehensive Guide to the Plays, Playwrights, Players, and Playhouses of the United Kingdom and America, from the Earliest to the Present Times. By W. DAVENPORT ADAMS. (Uniform with BREWER'S "Reader's Handbook.") Crown 8vo, half-bound, 12s. 6d.   [*In preparation.*]

Dramatists, The Old. Crown 8vo, cloth extra, with Vignette Portraits, 6s. per Vol.

Ben Jonson's Works. With Notes Critical and Explanatory, and a Biographical Memoir by WM. GIFFORD. Edited by Colonel CUNNINGHAM. Three Vols.

Chapman's Works. Complete in Three Vols. Vol. I. contains the Plays complete, including the doubtful ones; Vol. II., the Poems and Minor Translations, with an Introductory Essay by ALGERNON CHAS. SWINBURNE; Vol. III., the Translations of the Iliad and Odyssey.

DRAMATISTS, THE OLD, *continued—*

Marlowe's Works. Including his Translations. Edited, with Notes and Introduction, by Col. CUNNINGHAM. One Vol.

Massinger's Plays. From the Text of WILLIAM GIFFORD. Edited by Col. CUNNINGHAM. One Vol.

Dyer. — The Folk - Lore of Plants. By T. F. THISELTON DYER, M.A., &c. Crown 8vo, cloth extra, 7s. 6d.   [*In preparation.*]

Early English Poets. Edited, with Introductions and Annotations, by Rev. A. B. GROSART, D.D. Crown 8vo, cloth boards, 6s. per Volume.

Fletcher's (Giles, B.D.) Complete Poems. One Vol.

Davies' (Sir John) Complete Poetical Works. Two Vols.

Herrick's (Robert) Complete Collected Poems. Three Vols.

Sidney's (Sir Philip) Complete Poetical Works. Three Vols.

Herbert (Lord) of Cherbury's Poems. Edited, with Introduction, by J. CHURTON COLLINS. Crown 8vo, parchment, 8s.

Edwardes (Mrs. A.), Novels by :

A Point of Honour. Post 8vo, illustrated boards, 2s.

Archie Lovell. Post 8vo, illust. bds., 2s. ; crown 8vo, cloth extra, 3s. 6d.

Eggleston.—Roxy: A Novel. By EDWARD EGGLESTON. Post 8vo, illust. boards, 2s. ; cr. 8vo, cloth extra, 3s. 6d.

Emanuel.—On Diamonds and Precious Stones: their History, Value, and Properties ; with Simple Tests for ascertaining their Reality. By HARRY EMANUEL, F.R.G.S. With numerous Illustrations, tinted and plain. Crown 8vo, cloth extra, gilt, 6s.

Englishman's House, The : A Practical Guide to all interested in Selecting or Building a House, with full Estimates of Cost, Quantities, &c. By C. J. RICHARDSON. Third Edition. Nearly 600 Illusts. Cr. 8vo, cl. ex., 7s.6d.

Ewald (Alex. Charles, F.S.A.), Works by :

Stories from the State Papers. With an Autotype Facsimile. Crown 8vo, cloth extra, 6s.

The Life and Times of Prince Charles Stuart, Count of Albany, commonly called the Young Pretender. From the State Papers and other Sources. New and Cheaper Edition, with a Portrait, crown 8vo, cloth extra, 7s. 6d.

Eyes, The.—How to Use our
Eyes, and How to Preserve Them. By
JOHN BROWNING, F.R.A.S., &c. With
37 Illustrations. Crown 8vo, 1s.; cloth,
1s. 6d.

Fairholt.—Tobacco: Its His-
tory and Associations; with an Account of the Plant and its Manu-
facture, and its Modes of Use in all
Ages and Countries. By F. W. FAIR-
HOLT, F.S.A. With Coloured Frontispiece and upwards of 100 Illustrations by the Author. Crown 8vo, cloth
extra, 6s.

Familiar Allusions: A Hand-
book of Miscellaneous Information;
including the Names of Celebrated
Statues, Paintings, Palaces, Country
Seats, Ruins, Churches, Ships, Streets,
Clubs, Natural Curiosities, and the
like. By WILLIAM A. WHEELER,
Author of "Noted Names of Fiction;"
and CHARLES G. WHEELER. Demy
8vo, cloth extra, 7s. 6d.

Faraday (Michael), Works by:
The Chemical History of a Candle:
Lectures delivered before a Juvenile
Audience at the Royal Institution.
Edited by WILLIAM CROOKES, F.C.S.
Post 8vo, cloth extra, with numerous
Illustrations, 4s. 6d.
On the Various Forces of Nature,
and their Relations to each other:
Lectures delivered before a Juvenile
Audience at the Royal Institution.
Edited by WILLIAM CROOKES, F.C.S.
Post 8vo, cloth extra, with numerous
Illustrations, 4s. 6d.

Fin-Bec. — The Cupboard
Papers: Observations on the Art of
Living and Dining. By FIN-BEC. Post
8vo, cloth limp, 2s. 6d.

Fitzgerald (Percy), Works by:
The Recreations of a Literary Man;
or, Does Writing Pay? With Re-
collections of some Literary Men,
and a View of a Literary Man's
Working Life. Cr. 8vo, cloth extra, 6s.
The World Behind the Scenes.
Crown 8vo, cloth extra, 3s. 6d.
Little Essays: Passages from the
Letters of CHARLES LAMB. Post
8vo, cloth limp, 2s. 6d.

Post 8vo, illustrated boards, 2s. each.
Bella Donna. | Never Forgotten.
The Second Mrs. Tillotson.
Polly.
Seventy-five Brooke Street.
The Lady of Brantome.

Fletcher's (Giles, B.D.) Com-
plete Poems: Christ's Victorie in
Heaven, Christ's Victorie on Earth,
Christ's Triumph over Death, and
Minor Poems. With Memorial-Intro-
duction and Notes by the Rev. A. B.
GROSART, D.D. Cr. 8vo, cloth bds., 6s.

Fonblanque.—Filthy Lucre: A
Novel. By ALBANY DE FONBLANQUE.
Post 8vo, illustrated boards, 2s.

Francillon (R. E.), Novels by:
Crown 8vo, cloth extra, 3s. 6d. each;
post 8vo, illust. boards, 2s. each.
Olympia. | Queen Cophetua.
One by One.
Esther's Glove. Fcap. 8vo, picture
cover, 1s.
A Real Queen. Cr. 8vo, cl. extra, 3s. 6d.

French Literature, History of.
By HENRY VAN LAUN. Complete in
3 Vols., demy 8vo, cl. bds., 7s. 6d. each.

Frere.—Pandurang Hari; or,
Memoirs of a Hindoo. With a Preface
by Sir H. BARTLE FRERE, G.C.S.I., &c.
Crown 8vo, cloth extra, 3s. 6d.; post
8vo, illustrated boards, 2s.

Friswell.—One of Two: A Novel.
By HAIN FRISWELL. Post 8vo, illustrated boards, 2s.

Frost (Thomas), Works by:
Crown 8vo, cloth extra, 3s. 6d. each.
Circus Life and Circus Celebrities.
The Lives of the Conjurers.
The Old Showmen and the Old
London Fairs.

Fry.—Royal Guide to the Lon-
don Charities, 1884–5. By HERBERT
FRY. Showing, in alphabetical order,
their Name, Date of Foundation, Ad-
dress, Objects, Annual Income, Chief
Officials, &c. Published Annually.
Crown 8vo, cloth, 1s. 6d.

Gardening Books:
A Year's Work in Garden and Green-
house: Practical Advice to Amateur
Gardeners as to the Management of
the Flower, Fruit, and Frame Garden.
By GEORGE GLENNY. Post 8vo, cloth
limp, 2s. 6d.
Our Kitchen Garden: The Plants we
Grow, and How we Cook Them.
By TOM JERROLD, Author of "The
Garden that Paid the Rent," &c.
Post 8vo, cloth limp, 2s. 6d.
Household Horticulture: A Gossip
about Flowers. By TOM and JANE
JERROLD. Illust. Post 8vo, cl. lp., 2s. 6d.
The Garden that Paid the Rent.
By TOM JERROLD. Fcap. 8vo, illus-
trated cover, 1s.; cloth limp, 1s. 6d.

Garrett.—The Capel Girls: A Novel. By EDWARD GARRETT. Post 8vo, illust.bds., 2s.; cr.8vo, cl.ex., 3s. 6d.

Gentleman's Magazine (The) for 1884. One Shilling Monthly. A New Serial Story, entitled "Philistia," by CECIL POWER, is now appearing. "Science Notes," by W. MATTIEU WILLIAMS, F.R.A.S., and "Table Talk," by SYLVANUS URBAN, are also continued monthly.

* \.* *Now ready, the Volume for* JANUARY *to* JUNE, 1884, *cloth extra, price* **8s. 6d.**; *Cases for binding,* **2s.** *each.*

German Popular Stories. Collected by the Brothers GRIMM, and Translated by EDGAR TAYLOR. Edited, with an Introduction, by JOHN RUSKIN. With 22 Illustrations on Steel by GEORGE CRUIKSHANK. Square 8vo, cloth extra, **6s. 6d.**; gilt edges, **7s. 6d.**

Gibbon (Charles), Novels by: Crown 8vo, cloth extra, **3s. 6d.** each; post 8vo, illustrated boards, **2s.** each.

Robin Gray.	Queen of the
For Lack of Gold.	Meadow.
What will the	In Pastures Green
World Say?	Braes of Yarrow.
In Honour Bound.	The Flower of the
In Love and War.	Forest. [lem.
For the King.	A Heart's Prob-

Post 8vo, illustrated boards, **2s.**
The Dead Heart.

Crown 8vo, cloth extra, **3s. 6d.** each.
The Golden Shaft.
Of High Degree.
Fancy Free.
Loving a Dream.

By Mead and Stream. Three Vols., crown 8vo. [*Shortly.*

Gilbert (William), Novels by: Post 8vo, illustrated boards, **2s.** each.
Dr. Austin's Guests.
The Wizard of the Mountain.
James Duke, Costermonger.

Gilbert (W. S.), Original Plays by: In Two Series, each complete in itself, price **2s. 6d.** each.

The FIRST SERIES contains—The Wicked World—Pygmalion and Galatea — Charity — The Princess — The Palace of Truth—Trial by Jury.

The SECOND SERIES contains—Broken Hearts—Engaged—Sweethearts—Gretchen—Dan'l Druce—Tom Cobb—H.M.S. Pinafore—The Sorcerer—The Pirates of Penzance.

Glenny.—A Year's Work in Garden and Greenhouse: Practical Advice to Amateur Gardeners as to the Management of the Flower, Fruit, and Frame Garden. By GEORGE GLENNY. Post 8vo, cloth limp, **2s. 6d.**

Godwin.—Lives of the Necro- mancers. By WILLIAM GODWIN. Post 8vo, cloth limp, **2s.**

Golden Library, The: Square 16mo (Tauchnitz size), cloth limp, **2s.** per volume.

Bayard Taylor's Diversions of the Echo Club.

Bennett's (Dr. W. C.) Ballad History of England.

Bennett's (Dr.) Songs for Sailors.

Byron's Don Juan.

Godwin's (William) Lives of the Necromancers.

Holmes's Autocrat of the Breakfast Table. With an Introduction by G. A. SALA.

Holmes's Professor at the Breakfast Table.

Hood's Whims and Oddities. Complete. All the original Illustrations.

Irving's (Washington) Tales of a Traveller.

Irving's (Washington) Tales of the Alhambra.

Jesse's (Edward) Scenes and Occupations of a Country Life.

Lamb's Essays of Elia. Both Series Complete in One Vol.

Leigh Hunt's Essays: A Tale for a Chimney Corner, and other Pieces. With Portrait, and Introduction by EDMUND OLLIER.

Mallory's (Sir Thomas) Mort d'Arthur: The Stories of King Arthur and of the Knights of the Round Table. Edited by B. MONTGOMERIE RANKING.

Pascal's Provincial Letters. A New Translation, with Historical Introduction and Notes,by T.M'CRIE,D.D.

Pope's Poetical Works. Complete.

Rochefoucauld's Maxims and Moral Reflections. With Notes, and Introductory Essay by SAINTE-BEUVE.

St. Pierre's Paul and Virginia, and The Indian Cottage. Edited, with Life, by the Rev. E. CLARKE.

Shelley's Early Poems, and Queen Mab. With Essay by LEIGH HUNT.

Shelley's Later Poems: Laon and Cythna, &c.

Shelley's Posthumous Poems, the Shelley Papers, &c.

GOLDEN LIBRARY, THE, *continued*—

Shelley's Prose Works, including A Refutation of Deism, Zastrozzi, St. Irvyne, &c.

White's Natural History of Selborne. Edited, with Additions, by THOMAS BROWN, F.L.S.

Golden Treasury of Thought, The: An ENCYCLOPÆDIA OF QUOTATIONS from Writers of all Times and Countries. Selected and Edited by THEODORE TAYLOR. Crown 8vo, cloth gilt and gilt edges, 7s. 6d.

Gordon Cumming (C. F.), Works by:

In the Hebrides. With Autotype Facsimile and numerous full-page Illustrations. Demy 8vo, cloth extra, 8s. 6d.

In the Himalayas and on the Indian Plains. With numerous Illustrations. Demy 8vo, cloth extra, 8s. 6d. *[Shortly.*

Graham. — The Professor's Wife: A Story. By LEONARD GRAHAM. Fcap. 8vo, picture cover, 1s.; cloth extra, 2s. 6d.

Greeks and Romans, The Life of the, Described from Antique Monuments. By ERNST GUHL and W. KONER. Translated from the Third German Edition, and Edited by Dr. F. HUEFFER. With 545 Illustrations. New and Cheaper Edition, demy 8vo, cloth extra, 7s. 6d.

Greenwood (James), Works by:

The Wilds of London. Crown 8vo, cloth extra, 3s. 6d.

Low-Life Deeps: An Account of the Strange Fish to be Found There. Crown 8vo, cloth extra, 3s. 6d.

Dick Temple: A Novel. Post 8vo, illustrated boards, 2s.

Guyot.—The Earth and Man; or, Physical Geography in its relation to the History of Mankind. By ARNOLD GUYOT. With Additions by Professors AGASSIZ, PIERCE, and GRAY; 12 Maps and Engravings on Steel, some Coloured, and copious Index. Crown 8vo, cloth extra, gilt, 4s. 6d.

Hair (The): Its Treatment in Health, Weakness, and Disease. Translated from the German of Dr. J. PINCUS. Crown 8vo, 1s.

Hake (Dr. Thomas Gordon), Poems by:

Maiden Ecstasy. Small 4to, cloth extra, 8s.

HAKE's (Dr. T. G.) POEMS, *continued*—

New Symbols. Crown 8vo, cloth extra, 6s.

Legends of the Morrow. Crown 8vo, cloth extra, 6s.

The Serpent Play. Crown 8vo, cloth extra, 6s.

Hall.—Sketches of Irish Character. By Mrs. S. C. HALL. With numerous Illustrations on Steel and Wood by MACLISE, GILBERT, HARVEY, and G. CRUIKSHANK. Medium 8vo, cloth extra, gilt, 7s. 6d.

Halliday.—Every-day Papers. By ANDREW HALLIDAY. Post 8vo, illustrated boards, 2s.

Handwriting, The Philosophy of. With over 100 Facsimiles and Explanatory Text. By DON FELIX DE SALAMANCA. Post 8vo, cloth limp, 2s. 6d.

Hanky-Panky: A Collection of Very Easy Tricks, Very Difficult Tricks, White Magic, Sleight of Hand, &c. Edited by W. H. CREMER. With 200 Illusts. Crown 8vo, cloth extra, 4s. 6d.

Hardy (Lady Duffus). — Paul Wynter's Sacrifice: A Story. By Lady DUFFUS HARDY. Post 8vo, illust. boards, 2s.

Hardy (Thomas).—Under the Greenwood Tree. By THOMAS HARDY, Author of "Far from the Madding Crowd." Crown 8vo, cloth extra, 3s. 6d.; post 8vo, illustrated bds., 2s.

Haweis (Mrs. H. R.), Works by:

The Art of Dress. With numerous Illustrations. Small 8vo, illustrated cover, 1s.; cloth limp, 1s. 6d.

The Art of Beauty. New and Cheaper Edition. Crown 8vo, cloth extra, with Coloured Frontispiece and Illustrations, 6s.

The Art of Decoration. Square 8vo, handsomely bound and profusely Illustrated, 10s. 6d.

Chaucer for Children: A Golden Key. With Eight Coloured Pictures and numerous Woodcuts. New Edition, small 4to, cloth extra, 6s.

Chaucer for Schools. Demy 8vo, cloth limp, 2s. 6d.

Haweis (Rev. H. R.).—American Humorists. Including WASHINGTON IRVING, OLIVER WENDELL HOLMES, JAMES RUSSELL LOWELL, ARTEMUS WARD, MARK TWAIN, and BRET HARTE. By the Rev. H. R. HAWEIS, M.A. Crown 8vo, cloth extra, 6s.

Hawthorne (Julian), Novels by.

Crown 8vo, cloth extra, 3s. 6d. each ; post 8vo, illustrated boards, 2s. each.

| Garth. | Sebastian Strome. |
| Ellice Quentin. | Dust. |

Prince Saroni's Wife.

Mrs. Gainsborough's Diamonds. Fcap. 8vo, illustrated cover, 1s. ; cloth extra, 2s. 6d.

Crown 8vo, cloth extra, 3s. 6d. each.

Fortune's Fool.

Beatrix Randolph. With Illustrations by A. FREDERICKS.

Mercy Holland, and other Stories. Three Vols., crown 8vo.   [*Shortly.*

IMPORTANT NEW BIOGRAPHY.

Hawthorne (Nathaniel) and

his Wife. By JULIAN HAWTHORNE. With 6 Steel-plate Portraits. Two Vols., crown 8vo, cloth extra, 24s.

[Twenty-five copies of an *Edition de Luxe*, printed on the best hand-made paper, large 8vo size, and with India proofs of the Illustrations, are reserved for sale in England, price 48s. per set. Immediate application should be made by anyone desiring a copy of this special and very limited Edition.]

Heath (F. G.). — My Garden

Wild, and What I Grew There. By FRANCIS GEORGE HEATH, Author of "The Fern World," &c. Crown 8vo, cl. ex., 5s. ; cl. gilt, gilt edges, 6s.

Helps (Sir Arthur), Works by :

Animals and their Masters. Post 8vo, cloth limp, 2s. 6d.

Social Pressure. Post 8vo, cloth limp, 2s. 6d.

Ivan de Biron: A Novel. Crown 8vo, cloth extra, 3s. 6d.; post 8vo, illustrated boards, 2s.

Heptalogia (The); or, The

Seven against Sense. A Cap with Seven Bells. Cr. 8vo, cloth extra, 6s.

Herbert.—The Poems of Lord

Herbert of Cherbury. Edited, with Introduction, by J. CHURTON COLLINS. Crown 8vo, bound in parchment, 8s.

Herrick's (Robert) Hesperides,

Noble Numbers, and Complete Collected Poems. With Memorial-Introduction and Notes by the Rev. A. B. GROSART, D.D., Steel Portrait, Index of First Lines, and Glossarial Index, &c. Three Vols., crown 8vo, cloth, 18s.

Hesse - Wartegg (Chevalier

Ernst von), Works by :

Tunis : The Land and the People. With 22 Illustrations. Crown 8vo, cloth extra, 3s. 6d.

The New South-West: Travelling Sketches from Kansas, New Mexico, Arizona, and Northern Mexico. With 100 fine Illustrations and Three Maps. Demy 8vo, cloth extra, 14s.   [*In preparation.*

Hindley (Charles), Works by :

Crown 8vo, cloth extra, 3s. 6d. each.

Tavern Anecdotes and Sayings : Including the Origin of Signs, and Reminiscences connected with Taverns, Coffee Houses, Clubs, &c. With Illustrations.

The Life and Adventures of a Cheap Jack. By One of the Fraternity. Edited by CHARLES HINDLEY.

Hoey.—The Lover's Creed.

By Mrs. CASHEL HOEY. With 12 Illustrations by P. MACNAB. Three Vols., crown 8vo.   [*Shortly.*

Holmes (O. Wendell), Works by :

The Autocrat of the Breakfast-Table. Illustrated by J. GORDON THOMSON. Post 8vo, cloth limp, 2s. 6d.; another Edition in smaller type, with an Introduction by G. A. SALA. Post 8vo, cloth limp, 2s.

The Professor at the Breakfast-Table ; with the Story of Iris. Post 8vo, cloth limp, 2s.

Holmes. — The Science of

Voice Production and Voice Preservation: A Popular Manual for the Use of Speakers and Singers. By GORDON HOLMES, M.D. Crown 8vo, cloth limp, with Illustrations, 2s. 6d.

Hood (Thomas):

Hood's Choice Works, in Prose and Verse. Including the Cream of the Comic Annuals. With Life of the Author, Portrait, and 200 Illustrations. Crown 8vo, cloth extra, 7s. 6d.

Hood's Whims and Oddities. Complete. With all the original Illustrations. Post 8vo, cloth limp, 2s.

Hood (Tom), Works by :

From Nowhere to the North Pole: A Noah's Arkæological Narrative. With 25 Illustrations by W. BRUNTON and E. C. BARNES. Square crown 8vo, cloth extra, gilt edges, 6s.

A Golden Heart: A Novel. Post 8vo, illustrated boards, 2s.

Hook's (Theodore) Choice Humorous Works, including his Ludicrous Adventures, Bons Mots, Puns and Hoaxes. With a New Life of the Author, Portraits, Facsimiles, and Illusts. Cr. 8vo, cl. extra, gilt, 7s. 6d.

Hooper.—The House of Raby: A Novel. By Mrs. GEORGE HOOPER. Post 8vo, illustrated boards, 2s.

Horne.—Orion: An Epic Poem, in Three Books. By RICHARD HENGIST HORNE. With Photographic Portrait from a Medallion by SUMMERS. Tenth Edition, crown 8vo, cloth extra, 7s.

Howell.—Conflicts of Capital and Labour, Historically and Economically considered: Being a History and Review of the Trade Unions of Great Britain, showing their Origin, Progress, Constitution, and Objects, in their Political, Social, Economical, and Industrial Aspects. By GEORGE HOWELL. Cr. 8vo, cloth extra, 7s. 6d.

Hugo. — The Hunchback of Notre Dame. By VICTOR HUGO. Post 8vo, illustrated boards, 2s.

Hunt.—Essays by Leigh Hunt. A Tale for a Chimney Corner, and other Pieces. With Portrait and Introduction by EDMUND OLLIER. Post 8vo, cloth limp, 2s.

Hunt (Mrs. Alfred), Novels by: Crown 8vo, cloth extra, 3s. 6d. each; post 8vo, illustrated boards, 2s. each.

Thornicroft's Model.
The Leaden Casket.
Self-Condemned.

Ingelow.—Fated to be Free: A Novel. By JEAN INGELOW. Crown 8vo, cloth extra, 3s. 6d.; post 8vo, illustrated boards, 2s.

Irish Wit and Humour, Songs of. Collected and Edited by A. PERCEVAL GRAVES. Post 8vo, cl. limp, 2s. 6d.

Irving (Washington), Works by: Post 8vo, cloth limp, 2s. each.
Tales of a Traveller.
Tales of the Alhambra.

Janvier.—Practical Keramics for Students. By CATHERINE A. JANVIER. Crown 8vo, cloth extra, 6s.

Jay (Harriett), Novels by. Each crown 8vo, cloth extra, 3s. 6d.; or post 8vo, illustrated boards, 2s.
The Dark Colleen.
The Queen of Connaught.

Jefferies (Richard), Works by:
Nature near London. Crown 8vo, cloth extra, 6s.
The Life of the Fields. Crown 8vo, cloth extra, 6s.

Jennings (H. J.), Works by:
Curiosities of Criticism. Post 8vo, cloth limp, 2s. 6d.
Lord Tennyson: A Biographical Sketch. Crown 8vo, cloth extra, 6s. [In the press.

Jennings (Hargrave). — The Rosicrucians: Their Rites and Mysteries. With Chapters on the Ancient Fire and Serpent Worshippers. By HARGRAVE JENNINGS. With Five full-page Plates and upwards of 300 Illustrations. A New Edition, crown 8vo, cloth extra, 7s. 6d.

Jerrold (Tom), Works by:
The Garden that Paid the Rent. By TOM JERROLD. Fcap. 8vo, illustrated cover, 1s.; cloth limp, 1s. 6d.
Household Horticulture: A Gossip about Flowers. By TOM and JANE JERROLD. Illust. Post 8vo, cl.1p., 2s.6d.
Our Kitchen Garden: The Plants we Grow, and How we Cook Them. By TOM JERROLD. Post 8vo, cloth limp, 2s. 6d.

Jesse.—Scenes and Occupations of a Country Life. By EDWARD JESSE. Post 8vo, cloth limp, 2s.

Jones (Wm., F.S.A.), Works by:
Finger-Ring Lore: Historical, Legendary, and Anecdotal. With over 200 Illusts. Cr. 8vo, cl. extra, 7s. 6d.
Credulities, Past and Present; including the Sea and Seamen, Miners, Talismans, Word and Letter Divination, Exorcising and Blessing of Animals, Birds, Eggs, Luck, &c. With an Etched Frontispiece. Crown 8vo, cloth extra, 7s. 6d.
Crowns and Coronations: A History of Regalia in all Times and Countries. With One Hundred Illustrations. Cr. 8vo, cloth extra, 7s. 6d.

Jonson's (Ben) Works. With Notes Critical and Explanatory, and a Biographical Memoir by WILLIAM GIFFORD. Edited by Colonel CUNNINGHAM. Three Vols., crown 8vo, cloth extra, 18s.; or separately, 6s. each.

Josephus, The Complete Works of. Translated by WHISTON. Containing both "The Antiquities of the Jews" and "The Wars of the Jews." Two Vols., 8vo, with 52 Illustrations and Maps, cloth extra, gilt, 14s.

Kavanagh.—The Pearl Fountain, and other Fairy Stories. By BRIDGET and JULIA KAVANAGH. With Thirty Illustrations by J. MOYR SMITH. Small 8vo, cloth gilt, 6s.

Kempt.—Pencil and Palette: Chapters on Art and Artists. By ROBERT KEMPT. Post 8vo, cloth limp, 2s. 6d.

Kingsley (Henry), Novels by: Each crown 8vo, cloth extra, 3s. 6d.; or post 8vo, illustrated boards, 2s.

Oakshott Castle. | Number Seventeen

Knight.—The Patient's Vade Mecum: How to get most Benefit from Medical Advice. By WILLIAM KNIGHT, M.R.C.S., and EDWARD KNIGHT, L.R.C.P. Crown 8vo, 1s.; cloth, 1s. 6d.

Lamb (Charles):

Mary and Charles Lamb: Their Poems, Letters, and Remains. With Reminiscences and Notes by W. CAREW HAZLITT. With HANCOCK's Portrait of the Essayist, Facsimiles of the Title-pages of the rare First Editions of Lamb's and Coleridge's Works, and numerous Illustrations. Crown 8vo, cloth extra, 10s. 6d.

Lamb's Complete Works, in Prose and Verse, reprinted from the Original Editions, with many Pieces hitherto unpublished. Edited, with Notes and Introduction, by R. H. SHEPHERD. With Two Portraits and Facsimile of Page of the "Essay on Roast Pig." Cr. 8vo, cloth extra, 7s. 6d.

The Essays of Elia. Complete Edition. Post 8vo, cloth extra, 2s.

Poetry for Children, and Prince Dorus. By CHARLES LAMB. Carefully reprinted from unique copies. Small 8vo, cloth extra, 5s.

Little Essays: Sketches and Characters. By CHARLES LAMB. Selected from his Letters by PERCY FITZGERALD. Post 8vo, cloth limp, 2s. 6d.

Lane's Arabian Nights, &c.:

The Thousand and One Nights: commonly called, in England, "THE ARABIAN NIGHTS' ENTERTAINMENTS." A New Translation from the Arabic, with copious Notes, by EDWARD WILLIAM LANE. Illustrated by many hundred Engravings on Wood, from Original Designs by WM. HARVEY. A New Edition, from a Copy annotated by the Translator, edited by his Nephew, EDWARD STANLEY POOLE. With a Preface by STANLEY LANE-POOLE. Three Vols., demy 8vo, cloth extra, 7s. 6d. each.

LANE'S ARABIAN NIGHTS, *continued*—

Arabian Society in the Middle Ages: Studies from "The Thousand and One Nights." By EDWARD WILLIAM LANE, Author of "The Modern Egyptians," &c. Edited by STANLEY LANE-POOLE. Cr. 8vo, cloth extra, 6s.

Lares and Penates; or, The Background of Life. By FLORENCE CADDY. Crown 8vo, cloth extra, 6s.

Larwood (Jacob), Works by:

The Story of the London Parks. With Illustrations. Crown 8vo, cloth extra, 3s. 6d.

Clerical Anecdotes. Post 8vo, cloth limp, 2s. 6d.

Forensic Anecdotes Post 8vo, cloth limp, 2s. 6d.

Theatrical Anecdotes. Post 8vo, cloth limp, 2s. 6d.

Leigh (Henry S.), Works by:

Carols of Cockayne. With numerous Illustrations. Post 8vo, cloth limp, 2s. 6d.

Jeux d'Esprit. Collected and Edited by HENRY S. LEIGH. Post 8vo, cloth limp, 2s. 6d.

Life in London; or, The History of Jerry Hawthorn and Corinthian Tom. With the whole of CRUIKSHANK's Illustrations, in Colours, after the Originals. Crown 8vo, cloth extra, 7s. 6d.

Linton (E. Lynn), Works by:

Post 8vo, cloth limp, 2s. 6d. each.
Witch Stories.
The True Story of Joshua Davidson.
Ourselves: Essays on Women.

Crown 8vo, cloth extra, 3s. 6d. each; post 8vo, illustrated boards, 2s. each.
Patricia Kemball.
The Atonement of Leam Dundas.
The World Well Lost.
Under which Lord?
With a Silken Thread.
The Rebel of the Family.
"My Love!"
Ione.

Locks and Keys.—On the Development and Distribution of Primitive Locks and Keys. By Lieut.-Gen. PITT-RIVERS, F.R.S. With numerous Illustrations. Demy 4to, half Roxburghe, 16s.

Longfellow:
Longfellow's Complete Prose Works.
Including "Outre Mer," "Hyperion," "Kavanagh," "The Poets and Poetry of Europe," and "Driftwood." With Portrait and Illustrations by VALENTINE BROMLEY. Crown 8vo, cloth extra, 7s. 6d.

Longfellow's Poetical Works. Carefully Reprinted from the Original Editions. With numerous fine Illustrations on Steel and Wood. Crown 8vo, cloth extra, 7s. 6d.

Long Life, Aids to: A Medical, Dietetic, and General Guide in Health and Disease. By N. E. DAVIES, L.R.C.P. Crown 8vo, 2s; cloth limp, 2s. 6d. [*Shortly.*

Lucy.—Gideon Fleyce: A Novel. By HENRY W. LUCY. Crown 8vo, cl. extra, 3s. 6d.; post 8vo, illust. bds., 2s.

Lusiad (The) of Camoens.
Translated into English Spenserian Verse by ROBERT FFRENCH DUFF. Demy 8vo, with Fourteen full-page Plates, cloth boards, 18s.

McCarthy (Justin, M.P.), Works by:
A History of Our Own Times, from the Accession of Queen Victoria to the General Election of 1880. Four Vols. demy 8vo, cloth extra, 12s. each.—Also a POPULAR EDITION, in Four Vols. cr. 8vo, cl. extra, 6s. each.
A Short History of Our Own Times. One Vol., crown 8vo, cloth extra, 6s.
History of the Four Georges. Four Vols. demy 8vo, cloth extra, 12s. each. [Vol. I. *in the press.*

Crown 8vo, cloth extra, 3s. 6d. each; post 8vo, illustrated boards, 2s. each.
Dear Lady Disdain.
The Waterdale Neighbours.
My Enemy's Daughter.
A Fair Saxon.
Linley Rochford
Miss Misanthrope.
Donna Quixote.
The Comet of a Season.

Maid of Athens. With 12 Illustrations by F. BARNARD. Crown 8vo, cloth extra, 3s. 6d.

McCarthy (Justin H., M.P.), Works by:
Serapion, and other Poems. Crown 8vo, cloth extra, 6s.
An Outline of the History of Ireland, from the Earliest Times to the Present Day. Cr. 8vo, 1s.; cloth, 1s. 6d.
England under Gladstone. Crown 8vo, cloth extra, 6s.

MacDonald (George, LL.D.), Works by:
The Princess and Curdle. With 11 Illustrations by JAMES ALLEN. Small crown 8vo, cloth extra, 5s.
Gutta-Percha Willie, the Working Genius. With 9 Illustrations by ARTHUR HUGHES. Square 8vo, cloth extra, 3s. 6d.
Paul Faber, Surgeon. With a Frontispiece by J. E. MILLAIS. Crown 8vo, cloth extra, 3s. 6d.; post 8vo, illustrated boards, 2s.
Thomas Wingfold, Curate. With a Frontispiece by C. J. STANILAND. Crown 8vo, cloth extra, 3s. 6d.; post 8vo, illustrated boards, 2s.

Macdonell.—Quaker Cousins: A Novel. By AGNES MACDONELL. Crown 8vo, cloth extra, 3s. 6d.; post 8vo, illustrated boards, 2s.

Macgregor. — Pastimes and Players. Notes on Popular Games. By ROBERT MACGREGOR. Post 8vo, cloth limp, 2s. 6d.

Maclise Portrait-Gallery (The) of Illustrious Literary Characters; with Memoirs—Biographical, Critical, Bibliographical, and Anecdotal—illustrative of the Literature of the former half of the Present Century. By WILLIAM BATES, B.A. With 85 Portraits printed on an India Tint. Crown 8vo, cloth extra, 7s. 6d.

Macquoid (Mrs.), Works by:
In the Ardennes. With 50 fine Illustrations by THOMAS R. MACQUOID. Square 8vo, cloth extra, 10s. 6d.
Pictures and Legends from Normandy and Brittany. With numerous Illustrations by THOMAS R. MACQUOID. Square 8vo, cloth gilt, 10s. 6d.
Through Normandy. With 90 Illustrations by T. R. MACQUOID. Square 8vo, cloth extra, 7s. 6d.
Through Brittany. With numerous Illustrations by T. R. MACQUOID. Square 8vo, cloth extra, 7s. 6d.
About Yorkshire. With 67 Illustrations by T. R. MACQUOID, Engraved by SWAIN. Square 8vo, cloth extra, 10s. 6d.
The Evil Eye, and other Stories. Crown 8vo, cloth extra, 3s. 6d.; post 8vo, illustrated boards, 2s.
Lost Rose, and other Stories. Crown 8vo, cloth extra, 3s. 6d.; post 8vo, illustrated boards, 2s.

Mackay.—Interludes and Un-
dertones: or, Music at Twilight. By
CHARLES MACKAY, LL.D. Crown 8vo,
cloth extra, 6s.

Magician's Own Book (The):
Performances with Cups and Balls,
Eggs, Hats, Handkerchiefs, &c. All
from actual Experience. Edited by
W. H. CREMER. With 200 Illustrations.
Crown 8vo, cloth extra, 4s. 6d.

Magic No Mystery: Tricks with
Cards, Dice, Balls, &c., with fully
descriptive Directions; the Art of
Secret Writing; Training of Perform-
ing Animals, &c. With Coloured
Frontispiece and many Illustrations.
Crown 8vo, cloth extra, 4s. 6d.

Magna Charta. An exact Facsimile of the Original in the British
Museum, printed on fine plate paper,
3 feet by 2 feet, with Arms and Seals
emblazoned in Gold and Colours.
Price 5s.

Mallock (W. H.), Works by:
The New Republic; or, Culture, Faith
and Philosophy in an English Country
House. Post 8vo, cloth limp, 2s. 6d.;
Cheap Edition, illustrated boards, 2s.
The New Paul and Virginia; or, Posi-
tivism on an Island. Post 8vo, cloth
limp, 2s. 6d.
Poems. Small 4to, bound in parch-
ment, 8s.
Is Life worth Living? Crown 8vo,
cloth extra, 6s.

Mallory's (Sir Thomas) Mort
d'Arthur: The Stories of King Arthur
and of the Knights of the Round Table.
Edited by B. MONTGOMERIE RANKING.
Post 8vo, cloth limp, 2s.

Marlowe's Works. Including
his Translations. Edited, with Notes
and Introduction, by Col. CUNNING-
HAM. Crown 8vo, cloth extra, 6s.

Marryat (Florence), Novels by:
Crown 8vo, cloth extra, 3s. 6d. each; or,
post 8vo, illustrated boards, 2s.
  Open! Sesame!
  Written in Fire.
Post 8vo, illustrated boards, 2s. each.
  A Harvest of Wild Oats.
  A Little Stepson.
  Fighting the Air.

Masterman.—Half a Dozen
Daughters: A Novel. By J. MASTER-
MAN. Post 8vo, illustrated boards, 2s.

Mark Twain, Works by:
The Choice Works of Mark Twain.
Revised and Corrected throughout by
the Author. With Life, Portrait, and
numerous Illustrations. Crown 8vo,
cloth extra, 7s. 6d.
The Adventures of Tom Sawyer.
Post 8vo, illustrated boards, 2s.
An Idle Excursion, and other Sketches.
Post 8vo, illustrated boards, 2s.
The Prince and the Pauper. With
nearly 200 Illustrations. Crown 8vo,
cloth extra, 7s. 6d.
The Innocents Abroad; or, The New
Pilgrim's Progress: Being some Ac-
count of the Steamship "Quaker
City's" Pleasure Excursion to
Europe and the Holy Land. With
234 Illustrations. Crown 8vo, cloth
extra, 7s. 6d. CHEAP EDITION (under
the title of "MARK TWAIN'S PLEASURE
TRIP"), post 8vo, illust. boards, 2s.
A Tramp Abroad. With 314 Illustra-
tions. Crown 8vo, cloth extra, 7s. 6d.;
Post 8vo, illustrated boards, 2s.
The Stolen White Elephant, &c.
Crown 8vo, cloth extra, 6s.; post 8vo,
illustrated boards, 2s.
Life on the Mississippi. With about
300 Original Illustrations. Crown
8vo, cloth extra, 7s. 6d.
The Adventures of Huckleberry
Finn. With numerous Illusts. Cr.
8vo, cloth extra, 7s. 6d. [*Preparing.*

Massinger's Plays. From the
Text of WILLIAM GIFFORD. Edited
by Col. CUNNINGHAM. Crown 8vo,
cloth extra, 6s.

Mayhew.—London Characters
and the Humorous Side of London
Life. By HENRY MAYHEW. With
numerous Illustrations. Crown 8vo,
cloth extra, 3s. 6d.

Mayfair Library, The:
Post 8vo, cloth limp, 2s. 6d. per Volume.
A Journey Round My Room. By
XAVIER DE MAISTRE. Translated
by HENRY ATTWELL.
Latter-Day Lyrics. Edited by W.
DAVENPORT ADAMS.
Quips and Quiddities. Selected by
W. DAVENPORT ADAMS.
The Agony Column of "The Times,"
from 1800 to 1870. Edited, with an
Introduction, by ALICE CLAY.
Balzac's "Comedie Humaine" and
its Author. With Translations by
H. H. WALKER.
Melancholy Anatomised: A Popular
Abridgment of "Burton's Anatomy
of Melancholy."

MAYFAIR LIBRARY, *continued—*

Gastronomy as a Fine Art. By BRILLAT-SAVARIN.

The Speeches of Charles Dickens.

Literary Frivolities, Fancies, Follies, and Frolics. By W. T. DOBSON.

Poetical Ingenuities and Eccentricities. Selected and Edited by W. T. DOBSON.

The Cupboard Papers. By FIN-BEC.

Original Plays by W. S. GILBERT. FIRST SERIES. Containing: The Wicked World — Pygmalion and Galatea — Charity — The Princess — The Palace of Truth—Trial by Jury.

Original Plays by W. S. GILBERT. SECOND SERIES. Containing: Broken Hearts — Engaged — Sweethearts — Gretchen—Dan'l Druce—Tom Cobb —H.M.S. Pinafore — The Sorcerer —The Pirates of Penzance.

Songs of Irish Wit and Humour. Collected and Edited by A. PERCEVAL GRAVES.

Animals and their Masters. By Sir ARTHUR HELPS.

Social Pressure. By Sir A. HELPS.

Curiosities of Criticism. By HENRY J. JENNINGS.

The Autocrat of the Breakfast-Table. By OLIVER WENDELL HOLMES. Illustrated by J. GORDON THOMSON.

Pencil and Palette. By ROBERT KEMPT.

Little Essays : Sketches and Characters. By CHAS. LAMB. Selected from his Letters by PERCY FITZGERALD.

Clerical Anecdotes. By JACOB LARWOOD.

Forensic Anecdotes; or, Humour and Curiosities of the Law and Men of Law. By JACOB LARWOOD.

Theatrical Anecdotes. By JACOB LARWOOD.

Carols of Cockayne. By HENRY S. LEIGH.

Jeux d'Esprit. Edited by HENRY S. LEIGH.

True History of Joshua Davidson. By E. LYNN LINTON.

Witch Stories. By E. LYNN LINTON.

Ourselves: Essays on Women. By E. LYNN LINTON.

Pastimes and Players. By ROBERT MACGREGOR.

The New Paul and Virginia. By W. H. MALLOCK.

The New Republic. By W. H. MALLOCK.

Puck on Pegasus. By H. CHOLMONDELEY-PENNELL.

MAYFAIR LIBRARY, *continued—*

Pegasus Re-Saddled. By H. CHOLMONDELEY-PENNELL. Illustrated by GEORGE DU MAURIER.

Muses of Mayfair. Edited by H. CHOLMONDELEY-PENNELL.

Thoreau: His Life and Aims. By H. A. PAGE.

Puniana. By the Hon. HUGH ROWLEY.

More Puniana. By the Hon. HUGH ROWLEY.

The Philosophy of Handwriting. By DON FELIX DE SALAMANCA.

By Stream and Sea. By WILLIAM SENIOR.

Old Stories Re-told. By WALTER THORNBURY.

Leaves from a Naturalist's Note-Book. By Dr. ANDREW WILSON.

Medicine, Family.—One Thousand Medical Maxims and Surgical Hints, for Infancy, Adult Life, Middle Age, and Old Age. By N. E. DAVIES, L.R.C.P. Lond. Cr. 8vo, 1s.; cl., 1s. 6d.

Merry Circle (The) : A Book of New Intellectual Games and Amusements. By CLARA BELLEW. With numerous Illustrations. Crown 8vo, cloth extra, 4s. 6d.

Mexican Mustang (On a). Through Texas, from the Gulf to the Rio Grande. A New Book of American Humour. By ALEX. E. SWEET and J. ARMOY KNOX, Editors of "Texas Siftings." 400 Illusts. Cr. 8vo, cloth extra, 7s. 6d.

Middlemass (Jean), Novels by: Touch and Go. Crown 8vo, cloth extra, 3s. 6d.; post 8vo, illust. bds., 2s. Mr. Dorillion. Post 8vo, illust. bds., 2s.

Miller.—Physiology for the Young; or, The House of Life: Human Physiology, with its application to the Preservation of Health. For use in Classes and Popular Reading. With numerous Illustrations. By Mrs. F. FENWICK MILLER. Small 8vo, cloth limp, 2s. 6d.

Milton (J. L.), Works by: The Hygiene of the Skin. A Concise Set of Rules for the Management of the Skin; with Directions for Diet, Wines, Soaps, Baths, &c. Small 8vo, 1s. ; cloth extra, 1s. 6d.

The Bath in Diseases of the Skin. Small 8vo, 1s. ; cloth extra, 1s. 6d.

The Laws of Life, and their Relation to Diseases of the Skin. Small 8vo, 1s. ; cloth extra, 1s. 6d.

Moncrieff. — The Abdication; or, Time Tries All. An Historical Drama. By W. D. SCOTT-MONCRIEFF. With Seven Etchings by JOHN PETTIE, R.A., W. Q. ORCHARDSON, R.A., J. MACWHIRTER, A.R.A., COLIN HUNTER, R. MACBETH, and TOM GRAHAM. Large 4to, bound in buckram, 21s.

Murray (D. Christie), Novels by. Crown 8vo, cloth extra, 3s. 6d. each; post 8vo, illustrated boards, 2s. each.

A Life's Atonement.
A Model Father.
Joseph's Coat.
Coals of Fire.
By the Gate of the Sea.

Crown 8vo, cloth extra, 3s. 6d. each.

Val Strange: A Story of the Primrose Way.
Hearts.
The Way of the World.

North Italian Folk. By Mrs. COMYNS CARR. Illust. by RANDOLPH CALDECOTT. Square 8vo, cloth extra, 7s. 6d.

Number Nip (Stories about), the Spirit of the Giant Mountains. Retold for Children by WALTER GRAHAME. With Illustrations by J. MOYR SMITH. Post 8vo, cloth extra, 5s.

Nursery Hints: A Mother's Guide in Health and Disease. By N. E. DAVIES, L.R.C.P. Crown 8vo, 1s.; cloth, 1s. 6d.

Oliphant. — Whiteladies: A Novel. With Illustrations by ARTHUR HOPKINS and HENRY WOODS. Crown 8vo, cloth extra, 3s. 6d.; post 8vo, illustrated boards, 2s.

O'Connor.—Lord Beaconsfield A Biography. By T. P. O'CONNOR, M.P. Sixth Edition, with a New Preface, bringing the book down to the Death of Lord Beaconsfield. Crown 8vo, cloth extra, 7s. 6d.

O'Reilly.—Phœbe's Fortunes: A Novel. With Illustrations by HENRY TUCK. Post 8vo, illustrated boards, 2s.

O'Shaughnessy (Arth.), Works by :

Songs of a Worker. Fcap. 8vo, cloth extra, 7s. 6d.
Music and Moonlight. Fcap. 8vo, cloth extra, 7s. 6d.
Lays of France. Crown 8vo, cloth extra, 10s. 6d.

Ouida, Novels by. Crown 8vo, cloth extra, 5s. each; post 8vo, illustrated boards, 2s. each.

Held in Bondage.	A Dog of Flanders.
Strathmore.	Pascarel.
Chandos.	Signa.
Under Two Flags.	In a Winter City.
Cecil Castlemaine's Gage.	Ariadne.
	Friendship.
Idalia.	Moths.
Tricotrin.	Pipistrello.
Puck.	A Village Commune.
Folle Farine.	
TwoLittleWooden Shoes.	Bimbi.
	In Maremma.

Wanda: A Novel. Crown 8vo, cloth extra, 5s.

Frescoes: Dramatic Sketches. Crown 8vo, cloth extra, 5s. [*Shortly.*

Bimbi: PRESENTATION EDITION. Sq. 8vo, cloth gilt, cinnamon edges, 7s. 6d.

Princess Napraxine. Three Vols., crown 8vo.

Wisdom, Wit, and Pathos. Selected from the Works of OUIDA by F. SYDNEY MORRIS. Small crown 8vo, cloth extra, 5s.

Page (H. A.), Works by :
Thoreau: His Life and Aims: A Study. With a Portrait. Post 8vo, cloth limp, 2s. 6d.

Lights on the Way: Some Tales within a Tale. By the late J. H. ALEXANDER, B.A. Edited by H. A. PAGE. Crown 8vo, cloth extra, 6s.

Pascal's Provincial Letters. A New Translation, with Historical Introduction and Notes, by T. M'CRIE, D.D. Post 8vo, cloth limp, 2s.

Patient's (The) Vade Mecum: How to get most Benefit from Medical Advice. By WILLIAM KNIGHT, M.R.C.S., and EDWARD KNIGHT, L.R.C.P. Crown 8vo, 1s.; cloth, 1s. 6d.

Paul Ferroll :
Post 8vo, illustrated boards, 2s. each.
Paul Ferroll: A Novel.
Why Paul Ferroll Killed his Wife.

Paul.—Gentle and Simple. By MARGARET AGNES PAUL. With a Frontispiece by HELEN PATERSON. Cr. 8vo, cloth extra, 3s. 6d.; post 8vo, illustrated boards, 2s.

Payn (James), Novels by.
Crown 8vo, cloth extra, 3s. 6d. each;
post 8vo, illustrated boards, 2s. each.

Lost Sir Massingberd.
The Best of Husbands.
Walter's Word.
Halves. | Fallen Fortunes.
What He Cost Her.
Less Black than we're Painted.
By Proxy. | High Spirits.
Under One Roof. | Carlyon's Year.
A Confidential Agent.
Some Private Views.
A Grape from a Thorn.
For Cash Only. | From Exile.

Post 8vo, illustrated boards, 2s. each.

A Perfect Treasure.
Bentinck's Tutor.
Murphy's Master.
A County Family. | At Her Mercy.
A Woman's Vengeance.
Cecil's Tryst.
The Clyffards of Clyffe.
The Family Scapegrace
The Foster Brothers.
Found Dead.
Gwendoline's Harvest.
Humorous Stories.
Like Father, Like Son.
A Marine Residence.
Married Beneath Him.
Mirk Abbey.
Not Wooed, but Won.
Two Hundred Pounds Reward.

Kit: A Memory. Crown 8vo, cloth
extra, 3s. 6d.

The Canon's Ward. With Portrait
of Author. Cr.8vo, cloth extra, 3s. 6d.

In Peril and Privation: A Book for
Boys. With numerous Illustra-
tions. Crown 8vo, cloth extra, 6s.
[In preparation.

Pennell (H. Cholmondeley),
Works by: Post 8vo, cloth limp,
2s. 6d. each.

Puck on Pegasus. With Illustrations.
The Muses of Mayfair. Vers de
Société, Selected and Edited by H.
C. PENNELL.
Pegasus Re-Saddled. With Ten full-
page Illusts. by G. DU MAURIER.

Phelps.—Beyond the Gates.
By ELIZABETH STUART PHELPS,
Author of "The Gates Ajar." Crown
8vo, cloth extra, 2s. 6d.

Pirkis.—Trooping with Crows:
A Story. By CATHERINE PIRKIS. Fcap.
8vo, picture cover, 1s.

Planché (J. R.), Works by:
The Cyclopædia of Costume; or,
A Dictionary of Dress—Regal, Ecclesiastical, Civil, and Military—from
the Earliest Period in England to the
Reign of George the Third. Including Notices of Contemporaneous
Fashions on the Continent, and a
General History of the Costumes of
the Principal Countries of Europe.
Two Vols., demy 4to, half morocco,
profusely Illustrated with Coloured
and Plain Plates and Woodcuts,
£7 7s. The Vols. may also be had
separately (each complete in itself)
at £3 13s. 6d. each: Vol. I. THE
DICTIONARY. Vol. II. A GENERAL
HISTORY OF COSTUME IN EUROPE.

The Pursuivant of Arms; or, Heraldry Founded upon Facts. With
Coloured Frontispiece and 200 Illustrations. Cr. 8vo, cloth extra, 7s. 6d.

Songs and Poems, from 1819 to 1879.
Edited, with an Introduction, by his
Daughter, Mrs. MACKARNESS. Crown
8vo, cloth extra, 6s.

Play-time: Sayings and Doings
of Baby-land. By EDWARD STANFORD.
Large 4to, handsomely printed in
Colours, 5s.

Plutarch's Lives of Illustrious
Men. Translated from the Greek,
with Notes Critical and Historical, and
a Life of Plutarch, by JOHN and
WILLIAM LANGHORNE. Two Vols.,
8vo, cloth extra, with Portraits, 10s. 6d.

Poe (Edgar Allan):—
The Choice Works, in Prose and
Poetry, of EDGAR ALLAN POE. With
an Introductory Essay by CHARLES
BAUDELAIRE, Portrait and Fac-
similes. Crown 8vo, cl. extra, 7s. 6d.

The Mystery of Marie Roget, and
other Stories. Post 8vo, illust.bds.,2s.

Pope's Poetical Works. Complete in One Vol. Post 8vo, cl. limp, 2s.

Power.—Philistia: A Novel. By
CECIL POWER. Three Vols., crown
8vo. *[Shortly.*

Price (E. C.), Novels by:
Valentina: A Sketch. With a Frontispiece by HAL LUDLOW. Cr. 8vo,
cl. ex., 3s. 6d.; post 8vo,illust. bds., 2s.

The Foreigners. Crown 8vo, cloth
extra, 3s. 6d.

Proctor (Richd. A.), Works by :

Flowers of the Sky. With 55 Illusts. Small crown 8vo, cloth extra, 4s. 6d.

Easy Star Lessons. With Star Maps for Every Night in the Year, Drawings of the Constellations, &c. Crown 8vo, cloth extra, 6s.

Familiar Science Studies. Crown 8vo, cloth extra, 7s. 6d.

Rough Ways made Smooth: A Series of Familiar Essays on Scientific Subjects. Cr. 8vo, cloth extra, 6s.

Our Place among Infinities: A Series of Essays contrasting our Little Abode in Space and Time with the Infinities Around us. Crown 8vo, cloth extra, 6s.

The Expanse of Heaven: A Series of Essays on the Wonders of the Firmament. Cr. 8vo, cloth extra, 6s.

Saturn and its System. New and Revised Edition, with 13 Steel Plates. Demy 8vo, cloth extra, 10s. 6d.

The Great Pyramid: Observatory, Tomb, and Temple. With Illustrations. Crown 8vo, cloth extra, 6s.

Mysteries of Time and Space. With Illusts. Cr. 8vo, cloth extra, 7s. 6d.

The Universe of Suns, and other Science Gleanings. With Illusts. Cr. 8vo, cloth extra, 7s. 6d. [*Shortly.*

Wages and Wants of Science Workers. Crown 8vo, 1s. 6d.

Pyrotechnist's Treasury (The); or, Complete Art of Making Fireworks. By THOMAS KENTISH. With numerous Illustrations. Cr. 8vo, cl. extra, 4s. 6d.

Rabelais' Works. Faithfully Translated from the French, with variorum Notes, and numerous characteristic Illustrations by GUSTAVE DORÉ. Crown 8vo, cloth extra, 7s. 6d.

Rambosson.—Popular Astronomy. By J. RAMBOSSON, Laureate of the Institute of France. Translated by C. B. PITMAN. Crown 8vo, cloth gilt, with numerous Illustrations, and a beautifully executed Chart of Spectra, 7s. 6d.

Reader's Handbook (The) of Allusions, References, Plots, and Stories. By the Rev. Dr. BREWER. Fourth Edition, revised throughout, with a New Appendix, containing a COMPLETE ENGLISH BIBLIOGRAPHY. Cr. 8vo, 1,400 pages, cloth extra, 7s. 6d.

Richardson. — A Ministry of Health, and other Papers. By BENJAMIN WARD RICHARDSON, M.D., &c. Crown 8vo, cloth extra, 6s.

Reade (Charles, D.C.L.), Novels by. Post 8vo, illustrated boards, 2s. each; or crown 8vo, cloth extra, Illustrated, 3s. 6d. each.

Peg Woffington. Illustrated by S. L. FILDES, A.R.A.

Christie Johnstone. Illustrated by WILLIAM SMALL.

It is Never Too Late to Mend. Illustrated by G. J. PINWELL.

The Course of True Love Never did run Smooth. Illustrated by HELEN PATERSON.

The Autobiography of a Thief; Jack of all Trades; and James Lambert. Illustrated by MATT STRETCH.

Love me Little, Love me Long. Illustrated by M. ELLEN EDWARDS.

The Double Marriage. Illust. by Sir JOHN GILBERT, R.A., and C. KEENE.

The Cloister and the Hearth. Illustrated by CHARLES KEENE.

Hard Cash. Illust. by F. W. LAWSON.

Griffith Gaunt. Illustrated by S. L. FILDES, A.R.A., and WM. SMALL.

Foul Play. Illust. by DU MAURIER.

Put Yourself in His Place. Illustrated by ROBERT BARNES.

A Terrible Temptation. Illustrated by EDW. HUGHES and A. W. COOPER.

The Wandering Heir. Illustrated by HELEN PATERSON, S. L. FILDES, A.R.A., CHARLES GREEN, and HENRY WOODS, A.R.A.

A Simpleton. Illustrated by KATE CRAUFORD.

A Woman-Hater. Illustrated by THOS. COULDERY.

Readiana. With a Steel-plate Portrait of CHARLES READE.

Singleheart and Doubleface: A Matter-of-fact Romance.

Good Stories of Men and other Animals.

The Jilt, and other Stories.

Riddell (Mrs. J. H.), Novels by : Crown 8vo, cloth extra, 3s. 6d. each; post 8vo, illustrated boards, 2s. each.

Her Mother's Darling.

The Prince of Wales's Garden Party.

Rimmer (Alfred), Works by :

Our Old Country Towns. With over 50 Illusts. Sq. 8vo, cloth gilt, 10s. 6d.

Rambles Round Eton and Harrow. 50 Illusts. Sq. 8vo, cloth gilt, 10s. 6d.

About England with Dickens. With 58 Illustrations by ALFRED RIMMER and C. A. VANDERHOOF. Square 8vo, cloth gilt, 10s. 6d.

Robinson (F. W.), Novels by:

Women are Strange. Cr. 8vo, cloth extra, 3s. 6d.; post 8vo, illust. bds., 2s.

The Hands of Justice. Crown 8vo, cloth extra, 3s. 6d.

Robinson (Phil), Works by:

The Poets' Birds. Crown 8vo, cloth extra, 7s. 6d.

The Poets' Beasts. Crown 8vo, cloth extra, 7s. 6d. [*In preparation.*

Robinson Crusoe: A beautiful

reproduction of Major's Edition, with 37 Woodcuts and Two Steel Plates by GEORGE CRUIKSHANK, choicely printed. Crown 8vo, cloth extra, 7s. 6d. A few Large-Paper copies, printed on hand-made paper, with India proofs of the Illustrations, price 36s.

Rochefoucauld's Maxims and

Moral Reflections. With Notes, and an Introductory Essay by SAINTE-BEUVE. Post 8vo, cloth limp, 2s.

Roll of Battle Abbey, The; or,

A List of the Principal Warriors who came over from Normandy with William the Conqueror, and Settled in this Country, A.D. 1066-7. With the principal Arms emblazoned in Gold and Colours. Handsomely printed, price 5s.

Rowley (Hon. Hugh), Works by:

Post 8vo, cloth limp, 2s. 6d. each.

Puniana: Riddles and Jokes. With numerous Illustrations.

More Puniana. Profusely Illustrated.

Russell (Clark).—Round the

Galley-Fire. By W. CLARK RUSSELL, Author of "The Wreck of the *Grosvenor.*" Cr. 8vo, cloth extra, 6s.

Sala.—Gaslight and Daylight.

By GEORGE AUGUSTUS SALA. Post 8vo, illustrated boards, 2s.

Sanson.—Seven Generations

of Executioners: Memoirs of the Sanson Family (1688 to 1847). Edited by HENRY SANSON. Crown 8vo, cloth extra, 3s. 6d.

Saunders (John), Novels by:

Crown 8vo, cloth extra, 3s. 6d. each; post 8vo, illustrated boards, 2s. each.

Bound to the Wheel.

One Against the World.

Guy Waterman.

The Lion in the Path.

The Two Dreamers.

Saunders (Katharine), Novels by:

Crown 8vo, cloth extra, 3s. 6d. each.

Joan Merryweather.

Margaret and Elizabeth.

Gideon's Rock.

The High Mills.

Heart Salvage, by Sea and Land. Three Vols., crown 8vo.

Science Gossip: An Illustrated

Medium of Interchange for Students and Lovers of Nature. Edited by J. E. TAYLOR, F.L.S., &c. Devoted to Geology, Botany, Physiology, Chemistry, Zoology, Microscopy, Telescopy. Physiography, &c. Price 4d. Monthly; or 5s. per year, post free. Each Number contains a Coloured Plate and numerous Woodcuts. Vols. I. to XIV. may be had at 7s. 6d. each; and Vols. XV. to XIX. (1883). at 5s. each. Cases for Binding, 1s. 6d each.

Scott's (Sir Walter) Marmion.

An entirely New Edition of this famous and popular Poem, with over 100 new Illustrations by leading Artists. Elegantly and appropriately bound, small 4to, cloth extra, 16s.

[The immediate success of "The Lady of the Lake," published in 1882, has encouraged Messrs. CHATTO and WINDUS to bring out a Companion Edition of this not less popular and famous poem. Produced in the same style, and with the same careful and elaborate style of illustration, regardless of cost, Mr. Anthony's skilful supervision is sufficient guarantee that the work is elegant and tasteful as well as correct.]

"Secret Out" Series, The:

Crown 8vo, cloth extra, profusely Illustrated, 4s. 6d. each.

The Secret Out: One Thousand Tricks with Cards, and other Recreations; with Entertaining Experiments in Drawing-room or "White Magic." By W. H. CREMER. 300 Engravings.

The Pyrotechnist's Treasury; or, Complete Art of Making Fireworks. By THOMAS KENTISH. With numerous Illustrations.

The Art of Amusing: A Collection of Graceful Arts, Games, Tricks, Puzzles, and Charades. By FRANK BELLEW. With 300 Illustrations.

Hanky Panky: Very Easy Tricks, Very Difficult Tricks, White Magic, Sleight of Hand. Edited by W. H. CREMER. With 200 Illustrations.

"Secret Out" Series, *continued—*

The Merry Circle: A Book of New Intellectual Games and Amusements. By Clara Bellew. With many Illustrations.

Magician's Own Book: Performances with Cups and Balls, Eggs, Hats, Handkerchiefs, &c. All from actual Experience. Edited by W. H. Cremer. 200 Illustrations.

Magic No Mystery: Tricks with Cards, Dice, Balls, &c., with fully descriptive Directions; the Art of Secret Writing; Training of Performing Animals, &c. With Coloured Frontispiece and many Illustrations.

Senior (William), Works by :

Travel and Trout in the Antipodes. Crown 8vo, cloth extra, 6s.

By Stream and Sea. Post 8vo, cloth limp, 2s. 6d.

Seven Sagas (The) of Prehistoric Man. By James H. Stoddart, Author of "The Village Life." Crown 8vo, cloth extra, 6s.

Shakespeare :

The First Folio Shakespeare.—Mr. William Shakespeare's Comedies, Histories, and Tragedies. Published according to the true Originall Copies. London, Printed by Isaac Iaggard and Ed. Blount. 1623.—A Reproduction of the extremely rare original, in reduced facsimile, by a photographic process—ensuring the strictest accuracy in every detail. Small 8vo, half-Roxburghe, 7s. 6d.

The Lansdowne Shakespeare. Beautifully printed in red and black, in small but very clear type. With engraved facsimile of Droeshout's Portrait. Post 8vo, cloth extra, 7s. 6d.

Shakespeare for Children: Tales from Shakespeare. By Charles and Mary Lamb. With numerous Illustrations, coloured and plain, by J. Moyr Smith. Crown 4to, cloth gilt, 6s.

The Handbook of Shakespeare Music. Being an Account of 350 Pieces of Music, set to Words taken from the Plays and Poems of Shakespeare, the compositions ranging from the Elizabethan Age to the Present Time. By Alfred Roffe. 4to, half-Roxburghe, 7s.

A Study of Shakespeare. By Algernon Charles Swinburne. Crown 8vo, cloth extra, 8s.

Shelley's Complete Works, in Four Vols., post 8vo, cloth limp, 8s.; or separately, 2s. each. Vol. I. contains his Early Poems, Queen Mab, &c., with an Introduction by Leigh Hunt; Vol. II., his Later Poems, Laon and Cythna, &c.; Vol. III., Posthumous Poems, the Shelley Papers, &c.; Vol. IV., his Prose Works, including A Refutation of Deism, Zastrozzi, St. Irvyne, &c.

Sheridan :—

Sheridan's Complete Works, with Life and Anecdotes. Including his Dramatic Writings, printed from the Original Editions, his Works in Prose and Poetry, Translations, Speeches, Jokes, Puns, &c. With a Collection of Sheridaniana. Crown 8vo, cloth extra, gilt, with 10 full-page Tinted Illustrations, 7s. 6d.

Sheridan's Comedies: The Rivals, and The School for Scandal. Edited, with an Introduction and Notes to each Play, and a Biographical Sketch of Sheridan, by Brander Matthews. With Decorative Vignettes and 10 full-page Illustrations. Demy 8vo, cl. bds., 12s. 6d.

Short Sayings of Great Men. With Historical and Explanatory Notes by Samuel A. Bent, M.A. Demy 8vo, cloth extra, 7s. 6d.

Sidney's (Sir Philip) Complete Poetical Works, including all those in "Arcadia." With Portrait, Memorial-Introduction, Essay on the Poetry of Sidney, and Notes, by the Rev. A. B. Grosart, D.D. Three Vols., crown 8vo, cloth boards, 18s.

Signboards: Their History. With Anecdotes of Famous Taverns and Remarkable Characters. By Jacob Larwood and John Camden Hotten. Crown 8vo, cloth extra, with 100 Illustrations, 7s. 6d.

Sims (G. R.)—How the Poor Live. With 60 Illustrations by Fred. Barnard. Large 4to, 1s.

Sketchley.—A Match in the Dark. By Arthur Sketchley. Post 8vo, illustrated boards, 2s.

Slang Dictionary, The: Etymological, Historical, and Anecdotal. Crown 8vo, cloth extra, gilt, 6s. 6d.

Smith (J. Moyr), Works by :

The Prince of Argolis: A Story of the Old Greek Fairy Time. By J. Moyr Smith. Small 8vo, cloth extra, with 130 Illustrations, 3s. 6d.

SMITH'S (J. MOYR) WORKS, *continued*—
Tales of Old Thule. Collected and Illustrated by J. MOYR SMITH. Cr. 8vo, cloth gilt, profusely Illust., 6s.

The Wooing of the Water Witch: A Northern Oddity. By EVAN DALDORNE. Illustrated by J. MOYR SMITH. Small 8vo, cloth extra, 6s.

Spalding.—Elizabethan Demonology: An Essay in Illustration of the Belief in the Existence of Devils, and the Powers possessed by Them. By T. ALFRED SPALDING, LL.B. Crown 8vo, cloth extra, 5s.

Speight. — The Mysteries of Heron Dyke. By T. W. SPEIGHT. With a Frontispiece by M. ELLEN EDWARDS. Crown 8vo, cloth extra, 3s. 6d. ; post 8vo, illustrated boards, 2s.

Spenser for Children. By M. H. TOWRY. With Illustrations by WALTER J. MORGAN. Crown 4to, with Coloured Illustrations, cloth gilt, 6s.

Staunton.—Laws and Practice of Chess; Together with an Analysis of the Openings, and a Treatise on End Games. By HOWARD STAUNTON. Edited by ROBERT B. WORMALD. New Edition, small cr. 8vo, cloth extra, 5s.

Sterndale.—The Afghan Knife: A Novel. By ROBERT ARMITAGE STERNDALE. Cr. 8vo, cloth extra, 3s. 6d.; post 8vo, illustrated boards, 2s.

Stevenson (R. Louis), Works by:
Travels with a Donkey in the Cevennes. Frontispiece by WALTER CRANE. Post 8vo, cloth limp, 2s. 6d.
An Inland Voyage. With Front. by W. CRANE. Post 8vo, cl. lp., 2s. 8d.
Virginibus Puerisque, and other Papers. Crown 8vo, cloth extra, 6s.
Familiar Studies of Men and Books. Crown 8vo, cloth extra, 6s.
New Arabian Nights. Crown 8vo, cl. extra, 6s.; post 8vo, illust. bds., 2s.
The Silverado Squatters. With Frontispiece. Cr. 8vo, cloth extra, 6s.

St. John.—A Levantine Family. By BAYLE ST. JOHN. Post 8vo, illustrated boards, 2s.

Stoddard.—Summer Cruising in the South Seas. By CHARLES WARREN STODDARD. Illust. by WALLIS MACKAY. Crown 8vo, cl. extra, 3s. 6d.

St. Pierre.—Paul and Virginia, and The Indian Cottage. By BERNARDIN DE ST. PIERRE. Edited, with Life, by the Rev. E. CLARKE. Post 8vo, cloth limp, 2s.

Stories from Foreign Novelists. With Notices of their Lives and Writings. By HELEN and ALICE ZIMMERN; and a Frontispiece. Crown 8vo cloth extra, 3s. 6d.

Strutt's Sports and Pastimes of the People of England; including the Rural and Domestic Recreations, May Games, Mummeries, Shows, Processions, Pageants, and Pompous Spectacles, from the Earliest Period to the Present Time. With 140 Illustrations. Edited by WILLIAM HONE. Crown 8vo, cloth extra, 7s. 6d.

Suburban Homes (The) of London: A Residential Guide to Favourite London Localities, their Society, Celebrities, and Associations. With Notes on their Rental, Rates, and House Accommodation. With Map of Suburban London. Cr.8vo,cl.ex.,7s.6d.

Swift's Choice Works, in Prose and Verse. With Memoir, Portrait, and Facsimiles of the Maps in the Original Edition of "Gulliver's Travels." Cr. 8vo, cloth extra, 7s. 6d.

Swinburne (Algernon C.), Works by:
The Queen Mother and Rosamond. Fcap. 8vo, 5s.
Atalanta in Calydon. Crown 8vo, 6s.
Chastelard. A Tragedy. Cr. 8vo, 7s.
Poems and Ballads. FIRST SERIES. Fcap. 8vo, 9s. Also in crown 8vo, at same price.
Poems and Ballads. SECOND SERIES. Fcap. 8vo, 9s. Also in crown 8vo, at same price.
Notes on Poems and Reviews. 8vo,1s.
William Blake: A Critical Essay. With Facsimile Paintings. Demy 8vo, 16s.
Songs before Sunrise. Cr. 8vo, 10s.6d.
Bothwell: A Tragedy. Crown 8vo, 12s. 6d.
George Chapman: An Essay. Crown 8vo, 7s.
Songs of Two Nations. Cr. 8vo, 6s.
Essays and Studies. Crown 8vo, 12s.
Erechtheus: A Tragedy. Cr. 8vo, 6s.
Note of an English Republican on the Muscovite Crusade. 8vo, 1s.
A Note on Charlotte Bronte. Crown 8vo, 6s.
A Study of Shakespeare. Cr. 8vo, 8s.
Songs of the Springtides. Crown 8vo, 6s.
Studies in Song. Crown 8vo, 7s.
Mary Stuart: A Tragedy. Cr. 8vo, 8s.
Tristram of Lyonesse, and other Poems. Crown 8vo, 9s.
A Century of Roundels. Small 4to, cloth extra, 8s.

Symonds.—Wine, Women and Song: Mediæval Latin Students' Songs. Now first translated into English Verse, with an Essay by J. ADDINGTON SYMONDS. Small 8vo, parchment, 6s. A few LARGE PAPER COPIES, carefully printed on hand-made paper, price 21s.   [Preparing.

Syntax's (Dr.) Three Tours: In Search of the Picturesque, in Search of Consolation, and in Search of a Wife. With the whole of ROWLANDSON's droll page Illustrations in Colours and a Life of the Author by J. C. HOTTEN. Medium 8vo, cl. extra, 7s. 6d.

Taine's History of English Literature. Translated by HENRY VAN LAUN. Four Vols., small 8vo, cloth boards, 30s.—POPULAR EDITION, Two Vols., crown 8vo, cloth extra, 15s.

Taylor (Dr. J. E., F.L.S.), Works by:
The Sagacity and Morality of Plants: A Sketch of the Life and Conduct of the Vegetable Kingdom. With Coloured Frontispiece and 100 Illusts. Crown 8vo, cl. extra, 7s. 6d.
Our Common British Fossils: A Complete Handbook. With numerous Illustrations. Crown 8vo, cloth extra, 7s. 6d.   [Preparing.

Taylor's (Bayard) Diversions of the Echo Club: Burlesques of Modern Writers. Post 8vo, cl. limp, 2s.

Taylor's (Tom) Historical Dramas: "Clancarty," "Jeanne Darc," "'Twixt Axe and Crown," "The Fool's Revenge," "Arkwright's Wife," "Anne Boleyn," "Plot and Passion." One Vol., crown 8vo, cloth extra, 7s. 6d.
. The Plays may also be had separately, at 1s. each.

Tennyson (Lord): A Biographical Sketch. By H. J. JENNINGS. Crown 8vo, cloth extra, 6s.

Thackerayana: Notes and Anecdotes. Illustrated by Hundreds of Sketches by WILLIAM MAKEPEACE THACKERAY, depicting Humorous Incidents in his School-life, and Favourite Characters in the books of his every-day reading. With Coloured Frontispiece. Cr. 8vo, cl. extra, 7s. 6d.

Thomas (Bertha), Novels by. Crown 8vo, cloth extra, 3s. 6d. each; post 8vo, illustrated boards, 2s. each.
Cressida.
Proud Maisie.
The Violin-Player.

Thomas (M.).—A Fight for Life: A Novel. By W. MOY THOMAS. Post 8vo, illustrated boards, 2s.

Thomson's Seasons and Castle of Indolence. With a Biographical and Critical Introduction by ALLAN CUNNINGHAM, and over 50 fine Illustrations on Steel and Wood. Crown 8vo, cloth extra, gilt edges, 7s. 6d.

Thornbury (Walter), Works by
Haunted London. Edited by EDWARD WALFORD, M.A. With Illustrations by F. W. FAIRHOLT, F.S.A. Crown 8vo, cloth extra, 7s. 6d.
The Life and Correspondence of J. M. W. Turner. Founded upon Letters and Papers furnished by his Friends and fellow Academicians. With numerous Illusts. in Colours, facsimiled from Turner's Original Drawings. Cr. 8vo, cl. extra, 7s. 6d.
Old Stories Re-told. Post 8vo, cloth limp, 2s. 6d.
Tales for the Marines. Post 8vo, illustrated boards, 2s.

Timbs (John), Works by:
The History of Clubs and Club Life in London. With Anecdotes of its Famous Coffee-houses, Hostelries, and Taverns. With numerous Illustrations. Cr. 8vo, cloth extra, 7s. 6d.
English Eccentrics and Eccentricities: Stories of Wealth and Fashion, Delusions, Impostures, and Fanatic Missions, Strange Sights and Sporting Scenes, Eccentric Artists, Theatrical Folks, Men of Letters, &c. With nearly 50 Illusts. Crown 8vo, cloth extra, 7s. 6d.

Torrens. — The Marquess Wellesley, Architect of Empire. An Historic Portrait. By W. M. TORRENS, M.P. Demy 8vo, cloth extra, 14s.

Trollope (Anthony), Novels by: Crown 8vo, cloth extra, 3s. 6d. each; post 8vo, illustrated boards, 2s. each.
The Way We Live Now.
The American Senator.
Kept in the Dark.
Frau Frohmann.
Marion Fay.

Crown 8vo, cloth extra, 3s. 6d. each.
Mr. Scarborough's Family.
The Land-Leaguers.

Trollope(Frances E.),Novels by
Like Ships upon the Sea. Crown 8vo, cloth extra, 3s. 6d.; post 8vo, illustrated boards, 2s.
Mabel's Progress. Crown 8vo, cloth extra, 3s. 6d.
Anne Furness. Cr. 8vo, cl. ex., 3s. 6d.

Trollope (T. A.).—Diamond Cut
Diamond, and other Stories. By
THOMAS ADOLPHUS TROLLOPE. Crown
8vo, cloth extra, 3s. 6d.; post 8vo,
illustrated boards, 2s.

Tytler (Sarah), Novels by:
Crown 8vo, cloth extra, 3s. 6d. each;
post 8vo, illustrated boards, 2s. each.
What She Came Through.
The Bride's Pass.

Saint Mungo's City. Three Vols.,
crown 8vo.

Beauty and the Beast. Three Vols.,
crown 8vo. [*Shortly.*

Tytler (C. C. Fraser-). — Mis-
tress Judith: A Novel. By C. C.
FRASER-TYTLER. Crown 8vo, cloth
extra, 3s. 6d.

Van Laun.—History of French
Literature. By HENRY VAN LAUN.
Complete in Three Vols., demy 8vo,
cloth boards, 7s. 6d. each.

Villari. — A Double Bond : A
Story. By LINDA VILLARI. Fcap.
8vo, picture cover, 1s.

Walcott.— Church Work and
Life in English Minsters; and the
English Student's Monasticon. By the
Rev. MACKENZIE E. C. WALCOTT, B.D.
Two Vols., crown 8vo, cloth extra,
with Map and Ground-Plans, 14s.

Walford (Edw., M.A.), Works by:
The County Families of the United
Kingdom. Containing Notices of
the Descent, Birth, Marriage, Education, &c., of more than 12,000 dis-
tinguished Heads of Families, their
Heirs Apparent or Presumptive, the
Offices they hold or have held, their
Town and Country Addresses, Clubs,
&c. Twenty-fourth Annual Edition,
for 1884, cloth, full gilt, 50s.

The Shilling Peerage (1884). Con-
taining an Alphabetical List of the
House of Lords, Dates of Creation,
Lists of Scotch and Irish Peers,
Addresses, &c. 32mo, cloth, 1s.
Published annually.

The Shilling Baronetage (1884).
Containing an Alphabetical List of
the Baronets of the United Kingdom,
short Biographical Notices, Dates
of Creation, Addresses, &c. 32mo,
cloth, 1s. Published annually.

The Shilling Knightage (1884). Containing an Alphabetical List of the
Knights of the United Kingdom,
short Biographical Notices, Dates
of Creation, Addresses, &c. 32mo,
cloth, 1s. Published annually.

WALFORD'S (EDW., M.A.) WORKS, *con.*—
The Shilling House of Commons
(1884). Containing a List of all the
Members of the British Parliament,
their Town and Country Addresses,
&c. 32mo, cloth, 1s. Published
annually.

The Complete Peerage, Baronetage, Knightage, and House of
Commons (1884). In One Volume,
royal 32mo, cloth extra, gilt edges,
5s. Published annually.

Haunted London. By WALTER
THORNBURY. Edited by EDWARD
WALFORD, M.A. With Illustrations
by F. W. FAIRHOLT, F.S.A. Crown
8vo, cloth extra, 7s. 6d.

Walton and Cotton's Complete
Angler; or, The Contemplative Man's
Recreation; being a Discourse of
Rivers, Fishponds, Fish and Fishing,
written by IZAAK WALTON; and In-
structions how to Angle for a Trout or
Grayling in a clear Stream, by CHARLES
COTTON. With Original Memoirs and
Notes by Sir HARRIS NICOLAS, and
61 Copperplate Illustrations. Large
crown 8vo, cloth antique, 7s. 6d.

Wanderer's Library, The :
Crown 8vo, cloth extra, 3s. 6d. each.
Wanderings in Patagonia; or, Life
among the Ostrich Hunters. By
JULIUS BEERBOHM. Illustrated.

Camp Notes: Stories of Sport and
Adventure in Asia, Africa, and
America. By FREDERICK BOYLE.

Savage Life. By FREDERICK BOYLE.

Merrie England in the Olden Time.
By GEORGE DANIEL. With Illustrations by ROBT. CRUIKSHANK.

Circus Life and Circus Celebrities.
By THOMAS FROST.

The Lives of the Conjurers. By
THOMAS FROST.

The Old Showmen and the Old
London Fairs. By THOMAS FROST.

Low-Life Deeps. An Account of the
Strange Fish to be found there. By
JAMES GREENWOOD.

The Wilds of London. By JAMES
GREENWOOD.

Tunis: The Land and the People.
By the Chevalier de HESSE-WAR-
TEGG. With 22 Illustrations.

The Life and Adventures of a Cheap
Jack. By One of the Fraternity.
Edited by CHARLES HINDLEY.

The World Behind the Scenes. By
PERCY FITZGERALD.

Tavern Anecdotes and Sayings:
Including the Origin of Signs, and
Reminiscences connected with Ta-
verns, Coffee Houses, Clubs, &c.
By CHARLES HINDLEY. With Illusts.

WANDERER'S LIBRARY, THE, *continued*—

The Genial Showman: Life and Adventures of Artemus Ward. By E. P. HINGSTON. With a Frontispiece.

The Story of the London Parks. By JACOB LARWOOD. With Illustrations.

London Characters. By HENRY MAYHEW. Illustrated.

Seven Generations of Executioners: Memoirs of the Sanson Family (1688 to 1847). Edited by HENRY SANSON.

Summer Cruising in the South Seas. By CHARLES WARREN STODDARD. Illustrated by WALLIS MACKAY.

Warner.—A Roundabout Journey. By CHARLES DUDLEY WARNER, Author of "My Summer in a Garden." Crown 8vo, cloth extra, 6s.

Warrants, &c. :—

Warrant to Execute Charles I. An exact Facsimile, with the Fifty-nine Signatures, and corresponding Seals. Carefully printed on paper to imitate the Original, 22 in. by 14 in. Price 2s.

Warrant to Execute Mary Queen of Scots. An exact Facsimile, including the Signature of Queen Elizabeth, and a Facsimile of the Great Seal. Beautifully printed on paper to imitate the Original MS. Price 2s.

Magna Charta. An exact Facsimile of the Original Document in the British Museum, printed on fine plate paper, nearly 3 feet long by 2 feet wide, with the Arms and Seals emblazoned in Gold and Colours. Price 5s.

The Roll of Battle Abbey; or, A List of the Principal Warriors who came over from Normandy with William the Conqueror, and Settled in this Country, A.D. 1066-7. With the principal Arms emblazoned in Gold and Colours. Price 5s.

Weather, How to Foretell the, with the Pocket Spectroscope. By F. W. CORY, M.R.C.S. Eng., F.R.Met. Soc., &c. With 10 Illustrations. Crown 8vo, 1s.; cloth, 1s. 6d.

Westropp.—Handbook of Pottery and Porcelain; or, History of those Arts from the Earliest Period. By HODDER M. WESTROPP. With numerous Illustrations, and a List of Marks. Crown 8vo, cloth limp, 4s. 6d.

Whistler v. Ruskin: Art and Art Critics. By J. A. MACNEILL WHISTLER. Seventh Edition, square 8vo, 1s.

White's Natural History of Selborne. Edited, with Additions, by THOMAS BROWN, F.L.S. Post 8vo, cloth limp, 2s.

Williams (W. Mattieu, F.R.A.S.), Works by:

Science Notes. See the GENTLEMAN'S MAGAZINE. 1s. Monthly.

Science in Short Chapters. Crown 8vo, cloth extra, 7s. 6d.

A Simple Treatise on Heat. Crown 8vo, cloth limp, with Illusts., 2s. 6d.

The Chemistry of Cookery. Crown 8vo, cloth extra, 6s. [*In the press.*

Wilson (Dr. Andrew, F.R.S.E.), Works by:

Chapters on Evolution: A Popular History of the Darwinian and Allied Theories of Development. Second Edition. Crown 8vo, cloth extra, with 259 Illustrations, 7s. 6d.

Leaves from a Naturalist's Notebook. Post 8vo, cloth limp, 2s. 6d.

Leisure-Time Studies, chiefly Biological. Third Edition, with a New Preface. Crown 8vo, cloth extra, with Illustrations, 6s.

Winter (J. S.), Stories by:
Crown 8vo, cloth extra, 3s. 6d. each, post 8vo, illustrated boards, 2s. each.

Cavalry Life. | Regimental Legends.

Wood.—Sabina: A Novel. By Lady WOOD. Post 8vo, illust. bds., 2s.

Words, Facts, and Phrases: A Dictionary of Curious, Quaint, and Out-of-the-Way Matters. By ELIEZER EDWARDS. New and cheaper issue, cr. 8vo, cl. ex., 7s. 6d.; half-bound, 9s.

Wright (Thomas), Works by:

Caricature History of the Georges. (The House of Hanover.) With 400 Pictures, Caricatures, Squibs, Broadsides, Window Pictures, &c. Crown 8vo, cloth extra, 7s. 6d.

History of Caricature and of the Grotesque in Art, Literature, Sculpture, and Painting. Profusely Illustrated by F. W. FAIRHOLT, F.S.A. Large post 8vo, cl. ex., 7s.6d.

Yates (Edmund), Novels by:
Post 8vo, illustrated boards, 2s. each.
Castaway. | The Forlorn Hope. Land at Last.

NOVELS BY THE BEST AUTHORS.

Now in the press.

WILKIE COLLINS'S NEW NOVEL.
"I Say No." By WILKIE COLLINS.
Three Vols., crown 8vo.

Mrs. CASHEL HOEY'S NEW NOVEL
The Lover's Creed. By Mrs. CASHEL
HOEY, Author of "The Blossoming of
an Aloe," &c. With 12 Illustrations
by P. MACNAB. Three Vols., crown
8vo.

SARAH TYTLER'S NEW NOVEL.
Beauty and the Beast. By SARAH
TYTLER, Author of "The Bride's Pass,"
"Saint Mungo's City," "Citoyenne
Jacqueline," &c. Three Vols., cr. 8vo.

CHARLES GIBBON'S NEW NOVEL.
By Mead and Stream. By CHARLES
GIBBON, Author of "Robin Gray,"
"The Golden Shaft," "Queen of the
Meadow," &c. Three Vols., cr. 8vo.

ROBT. BUCHANAN'S NEW NOVEL.
Foxglove Manor. By ROBT. BUCHANAN,
Author of "The Shadow of the Sword,"
"God and the Man," &c. Three Vols.,
crown 8vo.

BASIL'S NEW NOVEL.
"The Wearing of the Green." By
BASIL, Author of "Love the Debt,"
"A Drawn Game," &c. Three Vols.,
crown 8vo.

*JULIAN HAWTHORNE'S NEW
STORIES.*
Mercy Holland, and other Stories. By
J. HAWTHORNE, Author of "Garth,"
"Beatrix Randolph," &c. Three Vols.,
crown 8vo.

NEW NOVEL BY CECIL POWER.
Philistia. By CECIL POWER. Three
Vols., crown 8vo.

THE PICCADILLY NOVELS.

Popular Stories by the Best Authors. LIBRARY EDITIONS, many Illustrated,
crown 8vo, cloth extra, 3s. 6d. each.

BY MRS. ALEXANDER.
Maid, Wife, or Widow?

BY W. BESANT & JAMES RICE.
Ready-Money Mortiboy.
My Little Girl.
The Case of Mr. Lucraft.
This Son of Vulcan.
With Harp and Crown.
The Golden Butterfly.
By Celia's Arbour.
The Monks of Thelema.
'Twas in Trafalgar's Bay.
The Seamy Side.
The Ten Years' Tenant.
The Chaplain of the Fleet.

BY WALTER BESANT.
All Sorts and Conditions of Men.
The Captains' Room.
All in a Garden Fair.

BY ROBERT BUCHANAN.
A Child of Nature.
God and the Man.
The Shadow of the Sword.
The Martyrdom of Madeline.
Love Me for Ever.
Annan Water.
The New Abelard.

BY MRS. H. LOVETT CAMERON.
Deceivers Ever.
Juliet's Guardian.

BY MORTIMER COLLINS.
Sweet Anne Page.
Transmigration.
From Midnight to Midnight.

MORTIMER & FRANCES COLLINS.
Blacksmith and Scholar.
The Village Comedy.
You Play me False.

BY WILKIE COLLINS.

Antonina.	New Magdalen.
Basil.	The Frozen Deep.
Hide and Seek.	The Law and the
The Dead Secret.	Lady.
Queen of Hearts.	The Two Destinies
My Miscellanies.	Haunted Hotel.
Woman in White.	The Fallen Leaves
The Moonstone.	Jezebel's Daughter
Man and Wife.	The Black Robe.
Poor Miss Finch.	Heart and Science
Miss or Mrs.?	

BY DUTTON COOK.
Paul Foster's Daughter

BY WILLIAM CYPLES.
Hearts of Gold.

BY ALPHONSE DAUDET.
Port Salvation.

BY JAMES DE MILLE.
A Castle in Spain.

BY J. LEITH DERWENT.
Our Lady of Tears. | Circe's Lovers.

PICCADILLY NOVELS, *continued—*
BY E. C. PRICE.
Valentina. | The Foreigners.

BY CHARLES READE, D.C.L.
It is Never Too Late to Mend.
Hard Cash. | Peg Woffington.
Christie Johnstone.
Griffith Gaunt.
The Double Marriage.
Love Me Little, Love Me Long.
Foul Play.
The Cloister and the Hearth.
The Course of True Love.
The Autobiography of a Thief.
Put Yourself in His Place.
A Terrible Temptation.
The Wandering Heir. | A Simpleton.
A Woman-Hater. | Readiana.

BY MRS. J. H. RIDDELL.
Her Mother's Darling.
Prince of Wales's Garden-Party.

BY F. W. ROBINSON.
Women are Strange.
The Hands of Justice.

BY JOHN SAUNDERS.
Bound to the Wheel.
Guy Waterman.
One Against the World.
The Lion in the Path.
The Two Dreamers.

BY KATHARINE SAUNDERS.
Joan Merryweather
Margaret and Elizabeth.
Gideon's Rock. | The High Mills.

PICCADILLY NOVELS, *continued—*
BY T. W. SPEIGHT.
The Mysteries of Heron Dyke.

BY R. A. STERNDALE.
The Afghan Knife.

BY BERTHA THOMAS.
Proud Maisie. | Cressida.
The Violin-Player.

BY ANTHONY TROLLOPE.
The Way we Live Now.
The American Senator.
Frau Frohmann.
Marion Fay.
Kept in the Dark.
Mr. Scarborough's Family.
The Land-Leaguers.

BY FRANCES E. TROLLOPE.
Like Ships upon the Sea.
Anne Furness.
Mabel's Progress.

BY T. A. TROLLOPE.
Diamond Cut Diamond.

By IVAN TURGENIEFF and Others.
Stories from Foreign Novelists.

BY SARAH TYTLER.
What She Came Through.
The Bride's Pass.

BY C. C. FRASER-TYTLER.
Mistress Judith.

BY J. S. WINTER.
Cavalry Life.
Regimental Legends.

CHEAP EDITIONS OF POPULAR NOVELS.
Post 8vo, illustrated boards, 2s. each.

BY EDMOND ABOUT.
The Fellah.

BY HAMILTON AÏDÉ.
Carr of Carrlyon. | Confidences.

BY MRS. ALEXANDER.
Maid, Wife, or Widow?

BY SHELSLEY BEAUCHAMP.
Grantley Grange.

BY W. BESANT & JAMES RICE.
Ready-Money Mortiboy.
With Harp and Crown.
This Son of Vulcan. | My Little Girl.
The Case of Mr. Lucraft.
The Golden Butterfly.
By Celia's Arbour.

By BESANT AND RICE, *continued—*
The Monks of Thelema.
'Twas in Trafalgar's Bay.
The Seamy Side.
The Ten Years' Tenant.
The Chaplain of the Fleet.

BY WALTER BESANT.
All Sorts and Conditions of Men.
The Captains' Room.

BY FREDERICK BOYLE.
Camp Notes. | Savage Life.

BY BRET HARTE.
An Heiress of Red Dog.
The Luck of Roaring Camp.
Californian Stories.
Gabriel Conroy. | Flip.

CHEAP POPULAR NOVELS, *continued—*

BY ROBERT BUCHANAN.
The Shadow of the Sword.
A Child of Nature.
God and the Man.
The Martyrdom of Madeline.
Love Me for Ever.

BY MRS. BURNETT.
Surly Tim.

BY MRS. LOVETT CAMERON.
Deceivers Ever. | Juliet's Guardian.

BY MACLAREN COBBAN.
The Cure of Souls.

BY C. ALLSTON COLLINS.
The Bar Sinister.

BY WILKIE COLLINS.

Antonina.	Miss or Mrs. ?
Basil.	The New Magda-
Hide and Seek.	len.
The Dead Secret.	The Frozen Deep.
Queen of Hearts.	Law and the Lady.
My Miscellanies.	The Two Destinies
Woman in White.	Haunted Hotel.
The Moonstone.	The Fallen Leaves.
Man and Wife.	Jezebel's Daughter
Poor Miss Finch.	The Black Robe.

BY MORTIMER COLLINS.
Sweet Anne Page.
Transmigration.
From Midnight to Midnight.
A Fight with Fortune.

MORTIMER & FRANCES COLLINS.
Sweet and Twenty. | Frances.
Blacksmith and Scholar.
The Village Comedy.
You Play me False.

BY DUTTON COOK.
Leo. | Paul Foster's Daughter.

BY J. LEITH DERWENT.
Our Lady of Tears.

BY CHARLES DICKENS.
Sketches by Boz.
The Pickwick Papers.
Oliver Twist.
Nicholas Nickleby.

BY MRS. ANNIE EDWARDES.
A Point of Honour. | Archie Lovell.

BY M. BETHAM-EDWARDS.
Felicia. | Kitty.

BY EDWARD EGGLESTON.
Roxy.

CHEAP POPULAR NOVELS, *continued—*

BY PERCY FITZGERALD.
Bella Donna. | Never Forgotten.
The Second Mrs. Tillotson.
Polly.
Seventy-five Brooke Street.
The Lady of Brantome.

BY ALBANY DE FONBLANQUE.
Filthy Lucre.

BY R. E. FRANCILLON.
Olympia. | Queen Cophetua.
One by One.

Prefaced by Sir H. BARTLE FRERE.
Pandurang Hari.

BY HAIN FRISWELL.
One of Two.

BY EDWARD GARRETT.
The Capel Girls.

BY CHARLES GIBBON.

Robin Gray.	Queen of the Mea-
For Lack of Gold.	dow.
What will the	In Pastures Green
World Say ?	The Flower of the
In Honour Bound.	Forest.
The Dead Heart.	A Heart's Problem
In Love and War.	The Braes of Yar-
For the King.	row.

BY WILLIAM GILBERT.
Dr. Austin's Guests.
The Wizard of the Mountain.
James Duke.

BY JAMES GREENWOOD.
Dick Temple.

BY ANDREW HALLIDAY.
Every-Day Papers.

BY LADY DUFFUS HARDY.
Paul Wynter's Sacrifice.

BY THOMAS HARDY.
Under the Greenwood Tree.

BY JULIAN HAWTHORNE.
Garth. | Sebastian Strome
Ellice Quentin. | Dust.
Prince Saroni's Wife.

BY SIR ARTHUR HELPS.
Ivan de Biron.

BY TOM HOOD.
A Golden Heart.

BY MRS. GEORGE HOOPER.
The House of Raby.

BY VICTOR HUGO.
The Hunchback of Notre Dame.

CHEAP POPULAR NOVELS, *continued—*

BY MRS. ALFRED HUNT.
Thornicroft's Model.
The Leaden Casket.
Self-Condemned.

BY JEAN INGELOW.
Fated to be Free.

BY HARRIETT JAY.
The Dark Colleen.
The Queen of Connaught.

BY HENRY KINGSLEY.
Oakshott Castle. | Number Seventeen

BY E. LYNN LINTON.
Patricia Kemball.
The Atonement of Leam Dundas.
The World Well Lost.
Under which Lord ?
With a Silken Thread.
The Rebel of the Family.
"My Love!"

BY HENRY W. LUCY.
Gideon Fleyce.

BY JUSTIN McCARTHY, M.P.
Dear Lady Disdain.
The Waterdale Neighbours.
My Enemy's Daughter.
A Fair Saxon.
Linley Rochford.
Miss Misanthrope.
Donna Quixote.
The Comet of a Season.

BY GEORGE MACDONALD.
Paul Faber, Surgeon.
Thomas Wingfold, Curate.

BY MRS. MACDONELL.
Quaker Cousins.

BY KATHARINE S. MACQUOID.
The Evil Eye. | Lost Rose.

BY W. H. MALLOCK.
The New Republic.

BY FLORENCE MARRYAT.
Open! Sesame! | A Little Stepson.
A Harvest of Wild | Fighting the Air.
Oats. | Written in Fire.

BY J. MASTERMAN.
Half-a-dozen Daughters.

BY JEAN MIDDLEMASS.
Touch and Go. | Mr. Dorillion.

CHEAP POPULAR NOVELS, *continued—*

BY D. CHRISTIE MURRAY.
A Life's Atonement.
A Model Father.
Joseph's Coat.
Coals of Fire.
By the Gate of the Sea.

BY MRS. OLIPHANT.
Whiteladies.

BY MRS. ROBERT O'REILLY.
Phœbe's Fortunes.

BY OUIDA.
Held in Bondage. TwoLittleWooden
Strathmore. Shoes.
Chandos. Signa.
Under Two Flags. In a Winter City.
Idalia. Ariadne.
Cecil Castle- Friendship.
maine. Moths.
Tricotrin. Pipistrello.
Puck. A Village Com-
Folle Farine. mune.
A Dog of Flanders. Bimbi.
Pascarel. In Maremma.

BY MARGARET AGNES PAUL.
Gentle and Simple.

BY JAMES PAYN.
Lost Sir Massing- | Like Father, Like
berd. | Son.
A Perfect Trea- | A Marine Resi-
sure. | dence.
Bentinck's Tutor. | Married Beneath
Murphy's Master. | Him.
A County Family. | Mirk Abbey.
At Her Mercy. | Not Wooed, but
A Woman's Ven- | Won.
geance. | £200 Reward.
Cecil's Tryst. | Less Black than
Clyffards of Clyffe | We're Painted.
The Family Scape- | By Proxy.
grace. | Under One Roof.
Foster Brothers. | High Spirits.
Found Dead. | Carlyon's Year.
Best of Husbands | A Confidential
Walter's Word. | Agent.
Halves. | Some Private
Fallen Fortunes. | Views.
What He Cost Her | From Exile.
Humorous Stories | A Grape from a
Gwendoline's Har- | Thorn.
vest. | For Cash Only.

BY EDGAR A. POE.
The Mystery of Marie Roget.

CHEAP POPULAR NOVELS, *continued—*

BY E. C. PRICE.
Valentina.

BY CHARLES READE.
It is Never Too Late to Mend.
Hard Cash.
Peg Woffington.
Christie Johnstone.
Griffith Gaunt.
Put Yourself in His Place.
The Double Marriage.
Love Me Little, Love Me Long.
Foul Play.
The Cloister and the Hearth.
The Course of True Love.
Autobiography of a Thief.
A Terrible Temptation.
The Wandering Heir.
A Simpleton.
A Woman-Hater.
Readiana.

BY MRS. J. H. RIDDELL.
Her Mother's Darling.
Prince of Wales's Garden Party.

BY F. W. ROBINSON.
Women are Strange.

BY BAYLE ST. JOHN
A Levantine Family.

BY GEORGE AUGUSTUS SALA.
Gaslight and Daylight.

BY JOHN SAUNDERS.
Bound to the Wheel.
One Against the World.
Guy Waterman.
The Lion in the Path.
Two Dreamers.

BY ARTHUR SKETCHLEY.
A Match in the Dark.

BY T. W. SPEIGHT.
The Mysteries of Heron Dyke.

BY R. A. STERNDALE.
The Afghan Knife.

BY R. LOUIS STEVENSON.
New Arabian Nights.

BY BERTHA THOMAS.
Cressida. | Proud Maisie.
The Violin-Player.

BY W. MOY THOMAS.
A Fight for Life.

CHEAP POPULAR NOVELS, *continued—*

BY WALTER THORNBURY.
Tales for the Marines.

BY T. ADOLPHUS TROLLOPE.
Diamond Cut Diamond.

BY ANTHONY TROLLOPE.
The Way We Live Now
The American Senator.
Frau Frohmann.
Marion Fay.
Kept in the Dark.

By FRANCES ELEANOR TROLLOPE
Like Ships upon the Sea.

BY MARK TWAIN.
Tom Sawyer.
An Idle Excursion.
A Pleasure Trip on the Continent of Europe.
A Tramp Abroad.
The Stolen White Elephant.

BY SARAH TYTLER.
What She Came Through.
The Bride's Pass.

BY J. S. WINTER.
Cavalry Life. | Regimental Legends

BY LADY WOOD.
Sabina.

BY EDMUND YATES.
Castaway. | The Forlorn Hope.
Land at Last.

ANONYMOUS.
Paul Ferroll.
Why Paul Ferroll Killed his Wife.

Fcap. 8vo, picture covers, 1s. each.
Jeff Briggs's Love Story. By BRET HARTE.
The Twins of Table Mountain. By BRET HARTE.
Mrs. Gainsborough's Diamonds. By JULIAN HAWTHORNE.
Kathleen Mavourneen. By Author of "That Lass o' Lowrie's."
Lindsay's Luck. By the Author of "That Lass o' Lowrie's."
Pretty Polly Pemberton. By the Author of "That Lass o' Lowrie's."
Trooping with Crows. By Mrs. PIRKIS.
The Professor's Wife. By LEONARD GRAHAM.
A Double Bond. By LINDA VILLARI.
Esther's Glove. By R. E. FRANCILLON.
The Garden that Paid the Rent. By TOM JERROLD.

www.ingramcontent.com/pod-product-compliance
Lightning Source LLC
Chambersburg PA
CBHW020939030726
47496CB00005B/1269